THE
ARMCHAIR
NATURALIST

THE
ARMCHAIR
NATURALIST

HOW TO BE GOOD AT NATURE
WITHOUT REALLY TRYING

— JOHNSON P. JOHNSON —

ICON BOOKS

Published in the UK in 2007 by
Icon Books Ltd, The Old Dairy,
Brook Road, Thriplow,
Cambridge SG8 7RG
email: info@iconbooks.co.uk
www.iconbooks.co.uk

Sold in the UK, Europe, South Africa and Asia
by Faber & Faber Ltd, 3 Queen Square,
London WC1N 3AU or their agents

Distributed in the UK, Europe, South Africa and Asia
by TBS Ltd, TBS Distribution Centre, Colchester Road
Frating Green, Colchester CO7 7DW

This edition published in Australia in 2007
by Allen & Unwin Pty Ltd,
PO Box 8500, 83 Alexander Street,
Crows Nest, NSW 2065

Distributed in Canada by
Penguin Books Canada,
90 Eglinton Avenue East, Suite 700,
Toronto, Ontario M4P 2YE

ISBN: 978-1840468-45-8

Typesetting and design by Simmons Pugh

Printed and bound in the UK by Clays of Bungay

Earth's crammed with heaven
And every common bush afire with God.

Elizabeth Barrett Browning

This book is dedicated to
Henri Dunsmuir, Alex McMinn, Sam, Charlie and
Adrian Bunn. And of course Thomas, who is a living
study in animal behaviour.

Wildlife is often a delicate and fragile thing, and should be treated with the utmost respect at all times. Even the most well-meaning of people can unwittingly destroy what they sought only to observe. Therefore, should you leave your armchair to view plants or animals in their natural habitats, please do take tremendous care to have as little impact on them and their environment as you can (after all, they have as much right to the world as we do). This includes adhering to the following basic guidelines:

- Do not collect animals or insects, or pick wild flowers.

- Keep to footpaths or bridleways to avoid trampling plants and disturbing the homes of animals.

- Never drop litter (or cigarette ends) – even if you believe it to be biodegradable.

- Keep dogs on a lead.

- Close gates behind you.

- Avoid damaging fences or walls – they almost always belong to someone and very often are there for the safety of animals.

- Try to walk, cycle or travel by public transport to your chosen destination rather than taking a car.

CONTENTS

FLOWERS

INSECTS

BIRDS

TREES

AMPHIBIANS

FISH

ODDS AND ENDS

Becoming the
Armchair Naturalist

The problem with Nature

Nature is daunting. Even on a brief country walk
there can appear to be so much of it. Trees, flowers,
weeds, birds, tiny rodents, pond life, it's all there
(and more), going about its business and largely
oblivious of your existence. This is fine if you are
happy to wander through it as blithely ignorant of
the little Song Thrush's name as it is of yours. If this
leaves you unsatisfied, however, and you decide to
make an effort to comprehend Nature's ways, it's all
too easy to fall at the first hurdle – for in order to
understand a living thing, you first have to identify
what it is you are looking at, and too often the
flowers all appear a uniform 'plant green' colour;
the trees are all just tree-shaped; the birds are a sort
of indeterminate brown; and the mammals are a
mere blur as they flee before you into the nearest
undergrowth.

If only everything came with its own clearly
printed name tag – preferably with its Latin name
underneath – identification would pose no difficul-
ties, but given that even the 'easy' bits of Nature
such as the common Blackbird are not what they
seem (neither the youngsters nor the females are
black but a muddy brown), throwing in the towel
can seem a very tempting option.

The good news

Nature is daunting but, by breaking it down into
manageable parts and having a few simple tricks up
your sleeve, it is possible to unlock its mysteries and

feel at home enough to know that a Crane may eat a Cranefly resting on a Cranesbill, but not the other way around.

Furthermore, while many plants and animals may, at first, seem indistinguishable from many other plants and animals, on closer inspection they often reveal tell-tale features and habits or take to habitats that make identification gratifyingly straightforward. For example, the casual observer may confuse Blue Tits with Great Tits, but once you learn the simple rule that the Blue Tit has a *blue* head, mistaking one for the other becomes an impossibility. Delving slightly deeper, few people realise that there are *two* sorts of Bluebells in Britain – native English ones and invading Spanish ones – and although there are several differences between them, the simplest way of telling them apart is to sniff them because, unlike the English variety, Spanish Bluebells have little or no scent.

There is further good news from the amphibian and reptile worlds: the commonest frogs, toads and lizards in Britain are, respectively, the Common Frog, the Common Toad and the Common Lizard, and what is more, all three look like you would imagine they *should* look like.

And so it goes on. Once you have learnt some of Nature's ways from the comfort of your armchair, you can step into any wood, meadow or garden, or onto any towpath, beach or riverbank, confident in the knowledge that there will be waiting for you there some plant or creature with whom you have become familiar through these pages.

In order to help you on your way as much as possible, this book outlines the first things you should know about each of over a hundred subjects, from how to see a Badger to how to predict the weather. The subjects are split into the following groups: Mammals, Flowers, Insects, Birds, Trees,

Amphibians, Fish and, most importantly, Odds and Ends.

To give you some instant knowledge, each subject comes with an Easy Nature box which includes one easy-to-master fact regarding the topic or a handy trick to help you get to know more about it.

There is also a *What you should say* section to enable you to say something erudite, witty or deeply wise about the matter in hand. This can also come in handy if you need to stall for time while you try to remember exactly what the difference is between a Weasel and a Stoat, for example (p. 34).

Finally, you will find a Glossary towards the back of the book which contains many of the specialised words that naturalists use. Don't worry about having to learn these – they'll just come naturally to you over time.

Of course, the only way of honing your new-found knowledge is to go outdoors and put it to the test. It is my hope that, once you have read this book and become one of the world's foremost Armchair Naturalists, going outside to unravel the secrets of Nature first-hand will be even more richly rewarding.

The most ancient Briton of English beasts

Despite what you might have learnt from your reading of the adventures of Rupert the Bear, not all Badgers are necessarily called Bill (nor even do they speak in rhyming couplets, which is a further disappointment). Furthermore, even those Badgers called Badger do not spend their lives trying to curb the excesses of Toad of Toad Hall. Indeed, the pity of it is that although there are about 300,000 Badgers in Britain, and every last one of them is instantly recognisable thanks to the creature's high profile in children's literature, many people go through their entire life without ever seeing one in the flesh.

*Eurasian Badger
(Meles meles)*

BADGER VOCABULARY

Male Badgers are called *boars*, while females are *sows*. Their offspring are *cubs*. They all live together in *setts*.

How to see a Badger

i.   At dusk, head for a forest but not one at the extremities of Scotland, on the Isle of Man, the Scilly Isles or the Channel Islands.

ii. Locate a sett.

iii. Don't go too near – Badgers will sense your presence and won't venture out.

iv. Make sure you're downwind – Badgers have an excellent sense of smell.

v. Wait silently – Badgers can hear pins dropping (so leave any pins at home).

What you should think about while waiting

The Badger is Britain's largest land carnivore and its claws make it a natural digging machine and prodigious fighter if attacked. Their average lifespan is just three years, although they have been known to live up to fifteen in the wild. The black-and-white facial markings are believed to be a warning sign to other creatures to back off. They are nocturnal and colour-blind and, unlike most species in Britain, have their own Act of Parliament, the Badgers Act 1973, which makes it illegal to mess with them in any way.

EASY NATURE

Just remember this:

The Eurasian Badger has simple-to-recall relatives in more exotic parts of the world, including the fearless snake-eating **Honey Badger** (so called because it also expropriates honey from bees), and the **Stink Badger** (which defends itself by emitting stinking juices from its anal glands).

- Edward Thomas (1878–1917), a poet killed in the First World War, described the Badger as 'The most ancient Briton of English beasts', and indeed Badger fossils dating back 250,000 years have been found in Britain.

- When first classified scientifically, Badgers were thought to be a type of Bear, whereas they're actually related to Weasels, Stoats and the like (p. 34).

- The old English word for a Badger is a Brock, a name that still lives on in places such as Brockenhurst and Broxbourne.

What you should say:

'Of course, there's still no compelling proof that they spread TB to cattle, you know.'

The mobile Bat

Sadly, the bat population has been in decline in Britain for the last few decades and hence is now protected by law. However, their habitats continue to be destroyed by developers, whether by accident or design, and the future of some species is in considerable doubt. As for identifying those bats that remain, differentiating between the seventeen British species is extremely difficult, since a typical encounter lasts only a matter of seconds in fading light and often ends before the realisation sinks in that a bat rather than a bird has just flown by. Thus, if you can squirrel away a few names of British bats and remember where you are most likely to see them, you give yourself at least some hope of guessing their identity. To improve your chances still further, you would be advised to join one of the many bat walks organised by nature conservancy groups.

Greater
Horseshoe
Bat

Bats you might see more or less anywhere in Britain

The **Common Pipistrelle** (*Pipistrellus pipistrellus*) is not only our commonest and smallest bat (3.3–5cm), but very nearly our smallest mammal to boot. It weighs a mere 5 grammes.

Until it was discovered, quite recently, that the echo location calls of the **Soprano Pipistrelle** (*Pipistrellus pygmaeus*) were even higher pitched than those of the Common Pipistrelle, no one knew that they were a different species. The two can still be told apart in flight only by the use of bat-detectors.

The **Brown Long-eared Bat** (*Plecotus auritus*) has fluffy brown fur on top and ears so large they are hilarious to everyone but their own mothers. **Daubenton's Bat** (*Myotis daubentoni*) is often found near water; while the **Natterer's Bat** (*Myotis nattereri*) has such broad wings that it is able to hover, if only for an instant.

Bats of England and Wales

The fluffy **Brandt's Bat** (*Myotis brandtii*) and the **Whiskered Bat** (*Myotis mystacinus*) were also thought to be one and the same until 1970. The **Common Noctule** (*Nyctalus noctula*) is Britain's largest bat, with a wingspan of up to 45cm. The **Barbastelle** (*Barbastella barbastellus*) is now, unhappily, extremely rare.

Bats of south Wales and south-west England

The **Greater Horseshoe Bat** (*Rhinolophus ferrumequinum*) and the **Lesser Horseshoe Bat** (*Rhinolophus hipposideros*) are so called because their noses (or strictly speaking their *noseleaves*) are like horseshoes, with the points turned uppermost.

Obscure Bats from the regions

Bechstein's Bat (*Myotis bechsteinii*): Wiltshire, Hampshire, Dorset and Somerset.
Serotine Bat (*Eptesicus serotinus*): south-east England and Cornwall.
Leisler's Bat (*Nyctalus leisleri*): within the London/Bristol/Leeds triangle.
Grey Long-eared Bat (*Plecotus austriacus*): Isle of Wight and the nether parts of Dorset and Hampshire.

EASY NATURE

Just remember this:
Bats are the only mammals that fly.

- Contrary to almost universal belief, bats are not, in fact, blind. Their eyesight is on a par with that enjoyed by humans.

What you should say when all else fails:
'Marvellous thing, echo location …
echo location … echo location.'

Cool for Cats

The British cat population is dominated, of course, by Domestic Cats (*Felis sylvestris catus*), of whom there are estimated to be around 6 million. Loveable though they are, the harsh truth is that these pets account for the destruction of a vast array of wildlife, including Voles, Mice and Slow Worms as well as birds. If owners were to attach bells to little Pusskin's collar, the death toll would at least be reduced, albeit not in the case of the Slow Worms. The native Wildcat, on the other hand, is a rare beast and is now confined to small areas of the Highlands of Scotland. There are also numerous reports of rather more exotic *felids* prowling the countryside, and it is as well to have something to say on these should the matter arise.

Wildcat

Recognition

The **Wildcat** (*Felis sylvestris grampia*) can easily be mistaken for the domestic tabby. To make matters more complicated, there's a deal of inter-breeding between Wildcats and feral cats (domestic cats gone wild, of which there are about 900,000 in Britain). However, unless you are in a remote part of the Highlands, assume that every tabby cat you see is or was someone's pet. For the record, the Wildcat is stockier than the domestic cat; owns a stubbier, bushier tail with dark rings on it; has grey-brown markings; and a dark brown stripe down its spine.

Other cats on the loose

The last few decades have thrown up thousands of reports of 'big cats' almost the length and breadth of Britain, often in the wake of complaints by farmers of unusually high losses of sheep. Probably the most notorious case is that of **The Beast of Bodmin**. Numerous alleged sightings of a large feline creature on Bodmin Moor were largely substantiated by the release in 1998 of a 20-second video. The footage clearly shows a black cat just over 1m long (admittedly not that large for a 'Beast'), which a local zoo curator believes to be a species of Wildcat thought to have become extinct in Britain over a century beforehand.

However, most other well-documented cases point to the presence of more obvious candidates such as escaped Leopards, Black Panthers (which are just melanistic Leopards), Pumas, Lynxes and Jungle Cats or their offspring.

Black Panther

EASY NATURE

Just remember this:
The proper name for a member of the Wildcat fraternity is a *felid*. Throw this word into any conversation on the subject and you will instantly be taken for an expert.

What you should say:
'Now, lets go through this again: exactly *what* sort of felid do you think you saw?'

What passing bells for these who die as Cattle?

Centuries of Cattle (*Bos taurus*) and Sheep (p. 46) farming have made the British countryside what it is today. The lush green fields that, despite creeping urbanisation, still cover a high proportion of the land, are home and feeding ground to millions of *ungulates* (a good word to remember if you can – it means 'hoofed animals'). The increasing industrialisation of farming has meant that many 'less productive' native breeds of cattle have died out or are on the endangered list as farmers concentrate on rearing the more profitable varieties in order to keep their businesses economically viable. This is a great pity, not only because of the resultant reduced bio-diversity, but also because it tends to make one farm look much like another. Admittedly, farmers have no responsibility to make their land look attractive for passers-by, but it's hard not to feel some sense of loss. The one consolation is that once you've mastered the handful of common breeds, you'll be able to identify the cattle in a good 80 per cent of fields.

A Guernsey

Beef herds

If the 'cows' in a field have no udders, you are looking at a beef herd. Britain's most popular animal reared for this purpose is the **Limousin**, with nearly 700,000 births recorded annually. These are the familiar rusty-brown bulls, often with white faces. An ancient breed, the 20,000-year-old paintings in the Lascaux caves in France show animals very similar to the modern Limousin.

The **Charolais** (over 300,000 births/annum) are stocky, woolly individuals who are white all over, a sort of Leeds United of the cattle world. The breed originates from Charolles in central France.

The next commonest is the all-black **Aberdeen Angus**, Britain's most popular native cattle breed; followed by the Swiss import, **Simmental**, which is brown with the odd patch of white.

Dairy herds

Eight in every ten cows currently ruminating in British fields are **Holstein Friesian**, a black-and-white breed from northern Germany and Holland, as their name suggests.

Other breeds fighting their corner include the **Jersey**, a more or less all-over fawn animal with a dark patch down the front of its head; the **Guernsey**, which has broadly the same markings as the Holstein Friesian but brown and white; and the **Ayrshire**, which looks very similar to the Guernsey but usually has less of a 'camouflaged' look to it.

EASY NATURE

Just remember this:

The image your mind's eye conjures up at the mention of the word 'cow' is in fact a very specific cow, the Holstein Friesian.

What you should say:

'Ah, the Guernsey – descended from two great French cattle breeds taken to the Channel Islands by militant monks in the 10th century, and a demned fine milker to boot.'

Dear Deer

There are six distinct species of deer running wild, or at least semi-wild, in Britain. Unfortunately, the thrill of coming across one is usually very short-lived, for most wild deer are afraid of humans (although Red Deer often seem less bothered). Vanishing, as if into thin air, is the deer's default defence mechanism – just try to get a second look at one you have surprised and which has subsequently found cover: it's an all but impossible task. It is therefore important to be able to identify deer in the few fleeting moments you are likely to enjoy before they disappear.

Red Deer (*Cervus elaphus*)

Look for: Red-brown coats (summer)/dark brown (winter).
Height to shoulder: To 1.3m.
Antlers (male only): Large.
Where: Scottish Highlands, southern Scotland, Lake District, south-west England (and famously in Richmond Park, London).

Sika Deer (*Cervus nippon*)

Look for: A white rump.
Colouring: Red-brown with white spots (summer)/very dark brown-blackish (winter).
Height to shoulder: To 90cm.
Antlers (male only): Medium.
Where: Scattered throughout England and Scotland.

Roe Deer (*Capreolus capreolus*)

Look for: A black band both sides of the nose that looks like a moustache.
Colouring: Red-brown (summer)/grey-brown (winter).
Height to shoulder: To 70cm.
Antlers (male only): Short.
Where: Hampshire, northern England, Scotland.

Fallow Deer (*Dama dama*)

Look for: Backs speckled with white (occasionally very dark with no dappling).
Colouring: Fawn.

Height to shoulder: To 1m.
Antlers (male only): Large.
Where: Throughout (except the far north of Scotland).

Reeves' Muntjac (*Muntiacus reevesi*)

Look for: Resembles a medium-sized dog.
Colouring: Light brown.
Height to shoulder: To 50cm.
Antlers (male only): Tiny.
Where: South and central England. Descendants from escapees from Woburn Park, to where they were brought from China in 1894.

Chinese Water Deer (*Hydropotes inermis*)

Look for: Eyes and nose like three big shiny black gobstoppers. Older animals develop tusks. Mainly nocturnal.
Colouring: Light buff (summer)/grey-brown (winter).
Height to shoulder: To 60cm.
Antlers: No.
Where: Descendants of escapees from Whipsnade Zoo – now ranging from Bedfordshire to Norfolk.

EASY NATURE

Just remember this:

The more points the antlers of a Red
or Sika Deer has, the older it is.

- Reindeer (*Rangifer tarandus*), which once used to roam wild in Britain, were reintroduced from Sweden in 1952 and are still farmed on the Cairngorms today.

- Male, female and young deer are bucks, does and fawns respectively, except in the case of the Red and Sika Deer, when they are referred to as stags, hinds and calves (while Reindeer are bulls, cows and calves).

What you should sing:

'Doe – a deer, a female deer.
Buck – its male counterpart.'

The hounded Fox

There's a bit of devilry about the Fox (*Vulpes vulpes*). Since the Middle Ages, and quite possibly long before then, they have been portrayed in folk stories, morality tales and even religious paintings as wily, cunning, untrustworthy animals. This perhaps explains why they tend to be blamed for far more losses of baby lambs than is their due.

As sinned against as sinning?

Certainly, let them into a roost and they will attempt to kill every last hen, an act that appears to amount to killing for the sake of it. However, if given the chance, they will bury the carcasses they cannot eat and dig them up later when food is hard to come by. Compare such behaviour with that of domestic cats, for example, who are renowned for their aptitude at killing their prey – often, it seems, deliberately slowly – without it ever occurring to them that they might want to eat it afterwards. Meanwhile, the poor Fox has endured centuries of being torn apart by hounds in the name of sport, and is reduced in many parts of an increasingly urbanised nation to scrounging its meals from dustbins. It may be that our false perception of the Fox lies with the fact that we expect them to behave like domestic dogs, and when they don't we are more outraged than we would be if they were some other wild animal for whom there is no pet equivalent.

Three things you should know about Foxes

i.   Vixens are fertile for just three days every year – in the depths of winter. To signal that she is on heat, she gives out a terrible squeal which sounds unnervingly like a human scream (the likeness has been used in a tedious number of murder mysteries as a way of introducing a red herring). The litter (usually up to six cubs) arrives about 51 days after conception.

ii. The British Fox population is estimated at several hundred thousand.

iii. They eat blackberries, which doesn't really fit with the image.

EASY NATURE

Just remember this:

Foxes live in *earths*, which are tunnels through earth (all right, and sometimes sand).

• 'Fox fires' is the colloquial term in Finland for the Aurora Borealis (or Northern Lights). The name comes either from the belief that the lights are caused by Foxes in the far north sweeping their brushes (tails) against banks of snow, or that a single Fox uses his brush to paint the sky. This is not the case. They are caused by material from the Sun colliding with the Earth's atmosphere.

• Foxes produce a pungent scent by means of something called a violet gland which is found on the top side of the brush. Shine an ultraviolet light on the secretions from this gland and you'll discover that they are fluorescent, though no one is sure quite why.

What you should say:

'The quick brown fox jumped over the lazy dog, or so I'm told.'

The return of the Goat

Although not native to Britain, Goats (*Capra hircus*) were introduced from the continent long before Julius Caesar arrived, and they have been kept as livestock ever since. That said, most goats you see on farms nowadays are breeds that came over from Switzerland as recently as the end of the 19th century. The few remaining 'British' domestic goats include such breeds as the **Golden Guernsey** and the **Bagot**. However, there are some scattered populations of feral goats that have established themselves after escapes from farms or deliberate releases, and spotting one is quite a treat.

A feral Goat

Questions you should ask yourself if you think you have seen a feral goat

i.   Is the goat in the Scottish Highlands, Snowdonia or the island of Lundy?

ii. Is it smaller and stockier than a farmed goat?

iii. Does its coat look rather shaggy and oily?

If the answer to all three is yes, it might well be that you have spotted a feral goat. Unfortunately, there are no further clues to be picked up with regard to their colouring, since they come in all shades of brown, grey, black and white, as do the domesticated breeds. Their horns also come in various shapes and sizes, including in the traditional 'swept-back' look.

GOAT LEXICOGRAPHY

For reasons best known to our forebears, English
has developed a special vocabulary when speaking
of the nuclear goat family:

nanny – a female goat

billy – a male goat

kid – a baby goat

EASY NATURE

Just remember this:

Male feral goats have larger horns
than female feral goats

- The term *scapegoat* comes from the annual Jewish celebration of Yom Kippur, wherein the sins of the nation were placed on two pure white goats. After lots were cast, one was sacrificed while the other – the scapegoat – was permitted to 'escape' into the wilderness with the burden of the sins on its back.

- The origins of the phrase 'get my goat' are uncertain, although it could be from defunct prison slang in which 'goat' meant 'anger'.

- The farming of dairy goats in Britain has experienced a revival in recent years due to the demand from the increasing number of people with an intolerance to cow's milk.

- Cashmere wool comes from the Cashmere Goat, as bred in Kashmir (and several other parts of Asia).

What you should say:

'Goats have a cartoon reputation for eating
everything that comes their way, but to be fair
to them they're really only keen on vegetation.
Indeed, they eat a lot of plants that are
poisonous to other grazing animals, so we
should all be jolly thankful.'

Hedgehogs, the one-trick wonders

There are no other species of mammal in Britain that have their own protective coating of spines (aside from any Porcupines and Echidnas lurking in zoos), so there is really no mistaking the Hedgehog. Furthermore, although other species of Hedgehog exist, the only one you'll find in Britain is the **European Hedgehog** (*Erinaceus europaeus*), which makes exact identification even simpler.

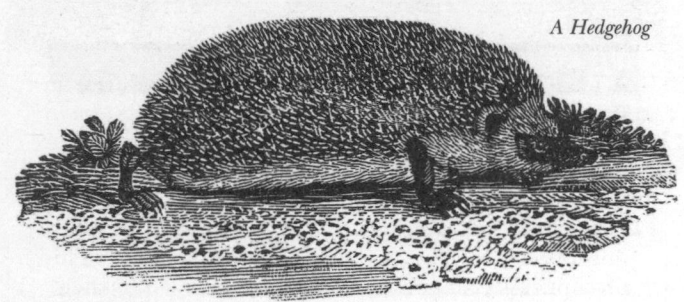

A Hedgehog

Seven things you should know about European Hedgehogs

i.   They are strictly nocturnal, so there is little point looking for them in daylight.

ii. The story that Hedgehogs have learnt to run out of the way of oncoming cars rather than rolling into a ball is, sadly, an urban myth.

iii. They eat Slugs, Earthworms and Beetles.

iv. Hibernation typically occurs from late October to early April.

v.   Each Hedgehog has several thousand spines, which are really hardened hairs.

vi. When in trouble, they make a sound like a pig squealing.

vii. They can swim (though prefer not to have to).

How to entice a Hedgehog to live in your garden

i.   Have a garden.

ii. Leave a corner as a 'wildlife sanctuary'.

iii. Provide nesting materials such as leaves, brushwood etc.

iv. Put out some cat food and a saucer of clean water,

preferably in a place with a small enough opening to stop cats getting in.

v. Make a nesting box with a low entrance tunnel (about 12cm high) and cover it with leaves, twigs and plastic sheeting.

vi. Take care never to disturb the box or Hedgehog nest, since this will almost certainly result in the swift departure of any Hedgehogs within.

The Injurious Incident of the Hedgehog on the Island

A few Hedgehogs were rather foolishly introduced to the Outer Hebrides in 1974 to deal with a slug problem in one of the islander's gardens. Twenty-five years later, a thriving population was playing havoc with the island's ground-nesting birds, whose eggs and offspring the Hedgehogs found delicious. Scottish Natural Heritage introduced a system of annual culls in 2002. This prompted a coalition of wildlife groups calling themselves Uist Hedgehog Rescue to start a programme of capturing the hedgehogs and relocating them on the mainland. The cull is currently suspended to see if shipping the little chaps off the island is a feasible solution. A similarly misguided Hedgehog introduction has been made on the Scilly Isles, though with less devastating effects.

EASY NATURE

Just remember this:

Hedgehogs steer clear of Badgers, which can eat them, so wherever you find Badgers you won't find Hedgehogs and vice versa.

What you should say:

'"Multa novit vulpes, verum echinus unum magnum", as Erasmus was wont to say.'[1]

---

[1]'The Fox has many tricks. The Hedgehog has but one. But that is the best of all.'

Going underground

The Mole is a remarkable creature in that, while it is one of the commonest mammals in Britain and nearly everyone is familiar with the sign of its presence – the famous 'mole hill' – very few people have actually ever seen one. For the record then, the **European Mole** (*Talpa europaea*) – the only mole species to inhabit British soil – is basically a cylinder covered with black fur. It's also much smaller than might be imagined from the size of the hillocks of earth it pushes up – the largest males grow to a modest 16cm in length with another 3 or 4cm of tail, while the females are even smaller.

A Mole

The interesting bits of a Mole

Its front feet – which are no more than digging machines on stalks.

Its long pink snout – through which the Mole detects prey (such as Earthworms and insect larvae). Moles have 44 teeth, which is an unusually high number for a mammal.

Its blindness – although born blind, European Moles can see (unlike the **Blind Mole** or the **Roman Mole**), albeit that their eyes are almost hidden by fur.

Spotting a Mole

This is not altogether a simple venture, given the creature's subterranean existence. However, you can maximise your chances by:

i. Conducting your search in spring, when males sometimes

come to the surface to seek out the burrows of females.

ii. Keeping your eyes peeled during extreme weather conditions – i.e. a summer drought when the ground has become very hard, or a period of wet weather in which the ground has been waterlogged – both of which could force Moles to seek refuge above ground

EASY NATURE

Just remember this:

Like Pigs (and Guinea Pigs), male Moles are *boars* while females are *sows*.

- The North American **Star-nosed Mole** (*Condylura cristata*) is on record as the world's fastest-eating mammal. It takes a mere 8 milliseconds on average to identify whether a particular prey is edible and, if it is, just another 112 milliseconds to capture and consume it.

- The earth pushed up into a mole hill is very good for potting up seedlings.

- Contrary to popular belief, the Mole does not hibernate.

- Happily, moleskin is not made of mole skin but is a cotton fabric with a pile on one side that is vaguely reminiscent of a mole's skin.

- Moleskine notebooks also have nothing to do with moleskins: they just happen to be made by an Italian company called Moleskine. Sighs of relief all round.

What you should say:

'The Mole may seem to you a humble sort of beast, but one once killed a king of England, you know.'[1]

---

[1] If asked for details, William III (1650–1702) died of pneumonia, a condition arising from a broken collar bone that he sustained falling from a horse that had stumbled on a mole hill. This led to the popular Jacobite toast to 'the little gentleman in the black velvet waistcoat'.

Sifting the Mustelids

The old playground joke about how to tell the difference between Weasels and Stoats is that while Weasels are weasely recognised, Stoats are stoatally different. If this were true, we'd all be happy. Sadly, not only can Weasels and Stoats be difficult to distinguish from each other (though the black tip of the Stoat's tail is the best indicator), there are three other similar-looking mammals scurrying around the British countryside: Polecats, Pine Martens and American Minks. While their distinctive long, sleek bodies make them easy to identify as some sort of Mustelid, being certain as to which is which is rather more problematical.

Do not lose heart. If you are sure you have seen a Mustelid, first consider where in Britain you are:

	Distribution
Weasel	Throughout mainland Britain
Stoat	Throughout mainland Britain plus Shetland
Polecat	Mainly in Wales and the West Midlands
Pine Marten	NW and far E of Scotland, pockets of N England and N Wales
American Mink	Everywhere except the far north of Scotland

NB i The only one of the five found in the Outer Hebrides is the American Mink.
NB ii The only one of the five found on the Isle of Man is the Stoat.
NB iii Only Weasels and Stoats have made it across to Anglesey.

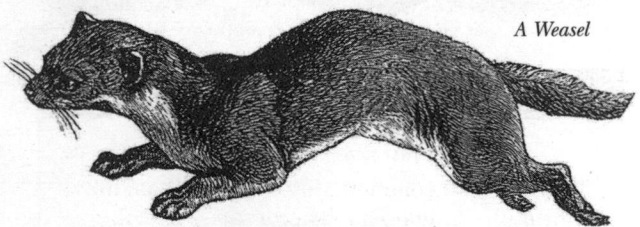

A Weasel

Next, bear in mind the countryside in which the animal was seen:

	Habitat
Weasel	Can live almost anywhere but prefers some ground cover
Stoat	Even more adaptable – can also live in marshes
Polecat	Farmland, marshland, the edges of woods and rivers
Pine Marten	Forests – favours deciduous or mixed woodland
American Mink	Lakes, ponds, sleepy rivers

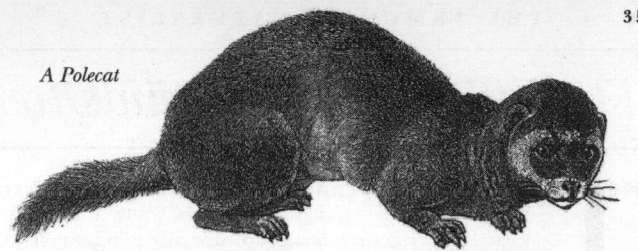

A Polecat

Once you have narrowed down the possibilities, concentrate on the colouring of the beast:

	Colour
Body/head	Gingery brown = Weasel
	Dull brown or white (in winter in Scotland) = Stoat
	Browny/yellow body and white patches on face = Polecat
	Dark brown (with big ears) = Pine Marten
	Almost black = American Mink
Throat	White = Weasel or Stoat
	Dark brown = Polecat
	A sort of orange blancmange colour = Pine Marten
	Almost black = American Mink

An American Mink

EASY NATURE

Just remember this:

There are two common Mustelids that thankfully bear very little resemblance to these five: the Badger (p. 16) and the Otter (p. 36).

- American Minks are the descendants of escapees from mink farms. Unfortunately, they have expressed their anger at their imprisonment by wiping out whole populations of Water Voles.

What you should say (to buy yourself some time):

'Look! There! My favourite Mustelid of all.'

The fall and rise of the Otter

There's something about an Otter – that flash of silver as it dives after an unwary fish; the astonishing grace and agility in the water, blended with an appealing awkwardness on land. And yet Britain's only species, the **European Otter** (*Lutra lutra*), all but came to grief in the 1970s, and was saved only by the intervention of some energetic conservationists (of which more below).

An Otter

Where Otters live

Otters are water-lovers and solitary creatures, each one living off a range of about 18km. It is a mistake, however, to imagine that they live only in rivers. For example, the coast of the Shetland Islands is home to fully 12 per cent of Britain's Otter population. (These are not, of course, to be confused with the **Sea Otters** (*Enhydra lutris*) of the North Pacific.)

Identification

Male Otters (dogs) grow up to 1.2m and females (bitches) 1m in length including their tails, making them much larger than other Mustelids like the Stoat and the Polecat (see p. 34). They have thick dark brown coats, off-white throats and under-sides, and webbed feet.

A conservation success story

Just a few decades ago, poisoned by farmers' pesticides and persecuted by anglers, the beleaguered Otter disappeared from large parts of the country. Thankfully, The Otter Trust came to the rescue, calling for a clean-up of rivers and streams, starting up an Otter breeding programme, and reintroducing the first Otters into the wild in 1983. 116 more Otters followed over the next sixteen years and, with tighter legislation on agricultural pollutants (and specifically, if you're taking notes, the organochlorine pesticides *Dieldrin* and *Aldrin*) and a 1981 Wildlife and Countryside Act protecting the species, numbers are now sufficiently buoyant to enable the Trust to discontinue its work. However, it is worth remembering that the European Otter is still on the IUCN Red List of Threatened Species (see p. 206), where it has been designated *Near Threatened* status.

EASY NATURE

Just remember this:

In the water, you can tell an Otter from similar creatures because only its head will break the surface while swimming.

- The novels *Tarka the Otter* by Henry Williamson and *Ring of Bright Water* by Gavin Maxwell both star European Otters.

- Otters can hold their breath for several minutes underwater.

- Otters mainly eat fish but won't turn their noses up at birds, small rodents or Sea Urchins.

What you should say:

'After a female gives birth to her litter, she bites her partner to make him go away. In so doing she averts the danger of him eating his own offspring in the belief that they are rats.'

They're short horses, aren't they?

Look up 'Pony' in a dictionary and you'll find a definition along the lines of: 'a breed of small horse, especially one lower than 14 hands 2 inches at the withers.' From this we can infer two things: i) 'Pony' is merely a convenient term for a small type of horse; and ii) it has *withers*. There are eight different breeds of wild or semi-wild Ponies (*Equus caballus*) in Britain, and since they are, in the main, tied to separate regions, they can be identified in nearly all cases by the simple expedient of knowing where they are (while keeping in mind that domesticated versions are produced in stud farms all around the country).

British Pony locations (from far north to south-west)

Shetland Pony: Shetland Islands

Highland Pony: Scottish Highlands

Dales Pony: East of the Pennines (mainly County Durham and Northumberland)

Fell Pony: Cumbria

Welsh Mountain Pony: Wales (especially Snowdonia)

New Forest Pony: New Forest, Hampshire

Exmoor Pony: Exmoor, Somerset/Devon

Dartmoor Pony: Dartmoor, Devon

How to measure a Pony

The height of a Pony is taken to be a perpendicular line from the ground to the top of the withers. The height is expressed in terms of *hands* and *inches*.

1. Do not attempt to measure the Pony by placing your hands one above the other up the poor animal's leg.
2. Measure the Pony instead with a stick or tape measure, in inches.
3. Convert the inches into hands and inches (there being four inches to a hand).

So, a typical **Exmoor Pony** measuring 50 inches is 12 *hands* 2 *inches* – written as 12.2hh (hands high) *not* 12.5hh.

COAT COLOURS

There's nothing that marks out a non-naturalist quicker than a weak grasp on jargon. The horse world (and, by extension, the Pony world) is full of it, particularly when it comes to colours:

Cremello: cream

Dun: a sort of beige

Palomino: gold

Bay: brown

Dappled grey: grey with large white speckles

Fleabitten grey: grey and white as if rendered by a Pointillist

Piebald: black and white

Skewbald: white and another colour (but not black)

Roan: white hairs over a base coat of a different colour (e.g. Blue Roan – a sort of metallic grey)

Blanket Appaloosa: a white section with dark speckles on the back or hind quarters

Chestnut: chestnut

EASY NATURE

Just remember this:
At under 10 hands, the Shetland is Britain's smallest Pony.

What you should say:

'Withers? Why, they're the highest point of a horse's back, just at the base of the neck and above the shoulders.'

Hare today gone tomorrow

The Rabbit is so much part and parcel of the countryside that the temptation is to ignore the creature completely in search of more exotic quarry. However, the budding naturalist should take advantage of the opportunities afforded by having a relatively tame wild mammal on their doorstep to hone their observation and tracking skills. These may then come in very useful when on the trail of the less numerous Brown Hare.

European Rabbit (*Oryctolagus cuniculus*)

Famously introduced by the Romans as a source of food, there are currently estimated to be around 40 million Rabbits in Britain. However, this figure is still well below the 100 million believed to have been present in the 1950s, when the virus Myxoma was deliberately released to deal with the 'Rabbit problem'. It succeeded beyond everyone's expectations, almost wiping out the entire population in 1953 via the slow death that is Myxomatosis. However, the million or so who survived bred like Rabbits – a healthy female can produce seven litters a year in theory – and total obliteration was averted.

Brown Hare (*Lepus europaeus*)

Once you have seen a Brown Hare, you will wonder how anyone could ever mistake it for a Rabbit. Not only is the creature a good deal larger, it has significantly longer ears and legs and, as a consequence of this latter trait, is a much faster runner to boot. Furthermore, Brown Hares do not live in warrens, but rather hunker down in a shallow pit called a form, often emerging only at dusk.

The spring boxing matches enacted by Brown Hares, which were once thought to be two males fighting over a female, have since been shown to be a female fighting off the attentions of an over-eager male, or at least playing hard to get.

Most pertinently, perhaps, the Brown Hare has suffered a dramatic drop in numbers due to loss of habitat brought about by changing farming methods. Where once the Brown Hare was a common sight, spotting one is fast becoming a rare treat.

The **Mountain** or **Blue Hare** (*Lepus timidus*) is examined in the section *Animals that turn white in winter* (p. 186).

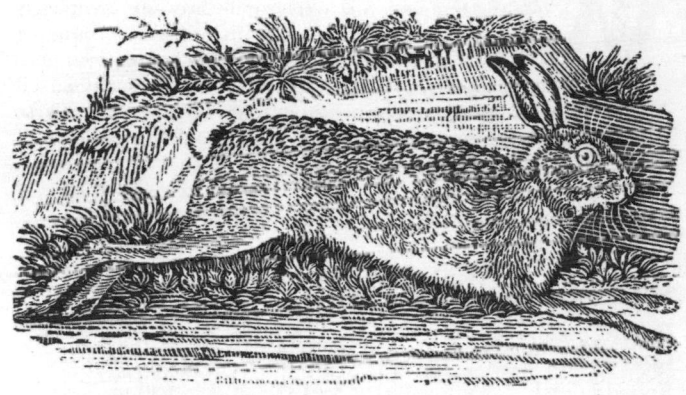

A Brown Hare

EASY NATURE

Just remember this:
Rabbits and Hares eat their
own pellets, though only once
– a process known as *refection*.

- Richard Adams' classic tale *Watership Down* is a more accurate depiction of wild Rabbit life and behaviour than you might imagine, since it was much influenced by *The Private Life of the Rabbit*, a seminal book on the subject by Welsh naturalist R.M. Lockley.

What you should say on encountering a sad Rabbit:
'Well *he's* not the happiest
bunny in the warren, is he?'

World of rodents

While it is true to say that members of the Rodentia order are not always everyone's favourite creatures, it behoves us to remember that they include such heart-melters as the **Hazel Dormouse**, the **Red Squirrel**, and that miniature acrobat of the wheaty stems, the **Harvest Mouse**. Indeed, once a person becomes aware of the sheer variety of rodents scurrying around outside (and, often enough, inside), the task of identifying more than a few may seem daunting.

A three-step programme for distinguishing one rodent from the next

Step 1 – Sort them into families

Unless you run across an escaped Hamster, you can concentrate on just three of the 30 families that make up the Rodentia order: Aplodontidae, Gliridae and Muridae. Squirrels are Aplodontidae; Dormice are Gliridae; everything else you might see is Muridae. If you've spotted a Squirrel or a Dormouse you can skip straight to Step 3.

Step 2 – Sort out the Muridae

This family has three main representatives in Britain: mice, voles and rats.

- Mice are small and skinny.
- Voles are also small but plumper, with shorter tails and rounder heads.
- Both British rats are much larger than any Mouse or Vole.

Step 3 – Sort out the species

Aplodontidae

Red Squirrels (*Sciurus vulgaris*) are smaller and very much rarer than **Grey Squirrels** (*Sciurus carolinensis*), and a reddy-brown to boot.

Gliridae

The tiny, gold-coated and endangered **Hazel Dormouse** (*Muscardinus avellanarius*) bears scant resemblance to the **Edible Dormouse** (*Glis glis*) which looks like a mini-Grey Squirrel, albeit with those familiar Dormouse shells for ears.

Muridae

Bank Voles (*Clethrionomys glareolus*) are medium-sized
(8–11cm) tree-climbers with a reddy-brown coat and long tail
(to 7cm). **Field Voles** (*Microtus agrestis*) are of similar size but
shorter in the tail (to 4cm) and greyer. **Water Voles** (*Arvicola
terrestris*) are much larger (to 22cm), dark brown doggy-
paddlers (when swimming), and often mistakenly referred to
as 'Water Rats' (an entirely fictitious creature).

The **Harvest Mouse** (*Micromys minutus*) is minute (5–8cm)
and found in fields. The **Wood Mouse** (*Apodemus sylvaticus*) is
Britain's commonest mouse, is medium-sized (8–11cm) and
lives in woods and more or less everywhere else (including
houses). The **House Mouse** (*Mus domesticus*) is fractionally
smaller (7–10cm) with noticeably smaller eyes and ears, and
is, after humans, the most widely distributed mammal in the
world. The **Yellow-necked Mouse** (*Apodemus flavicollis*) has an
obvious yellow band across its underside.

A House Mouse

The **Brown Rat** (*Rattus norvegicus*) is brown and common. The
Black Rat (*Rattus rattus*) is black, smaller and very rare.

EASY NATURE

Just remember this:
The Harvest Mouse is Britain's smallest mammal.

• On the Isle of Man it is considered unlucky to utter the word 'rat'.
The term 'Longtail' is used instead.

What you should say:
'The Grey Squirrel is but a rat with good PR.'

Seal of approval

There are only two sorts of seal around the British coast, so once you have convinced yourself that what you are looking at is a seal, you've a 50-50 chance of getting the right one. However, by memorising a few simple rules, it should be possible to tell them apart without resorting to guesswork.

Telling the difference between a Common Seal (*Phoca vitulina*) and a Grey Seal (*Halichoerus grypus*)

Pups

Fiendishly difficult, because pups of both species are a light mottled grey at birth and of similar size and build. Worse still, the species do not mix, so there is almost no chance of you ever coming across the two lying conveniently side by side eagerly awaiting the application of your forensic skills.

The key, as it turns out, is the nose. The nostril slits of a Grey Seal pup resemble the outer strokes of a 'W', whereas those of a Common Seal pup are closer together to form a far more definite 'V'. This is because the septum (the area in between the nostrils) is wider on a Grey Seal.

Adults

Both species are grey-brown with dark blotches on their backs, though the Common Seal can also be a much lighter grey. However, the Grey Seal is longer (bulls to 3.2m, cows to 2.4m) than the Common Seal (to 2m) and can weigh up to 300kg to a mere 120kg. Greys give out low moans (while Common Seals are practically silent), are much tamer, and are also wont to practise 'bottling' – remaining upright and motionless in the sea in order to have a good look around them. When all else fails, the aforementioned 'nostril test' can be applied. The difference in nose shape being that much more marked in adults, the test is foolproof if you have a good enough view of the seal's snout.

Grey Seals

EASY NATURE

Just remember this:
The Grey Seal is Britain's largest carnivore.

Where to see a Seal

Common Seals (also called Harbour Seals) can be found in many sheltered sections of the coastline of Scotland and eastern England. They particularly favour estuaries with sand banks on which they can bask. Grey Seals prefer rocky shorelines more or less anywhere around Britain except the long stretch from Devon to Norfolk.

- The Latin name for the Grey Seal, *Halichoerus grypus*, means 'sea pig with a hooked nose'.

- It has been discovered that seals often sleep out at sea, though usually not for longer than 90 seconds at a time.

What you should say:

'You can age a seal by counting the rings around the roots of the back teeth. Though I shouldn't try it with that big one, old chap.'

Some Sheep may safely graze

Difficult though it may be to believe, there are grassy swathes of Britain that play host to wild sheep. Admittedly, the sheep are confined to two islands – St Kilda (41 miles west of the Outer Hebrides) and Lundy (off the coast of Devon) – and their numbers are such that they are now an endangered species, but the fact of their existence is a pleasant surprise nonetheless. These **Soay Sheep** (*Ovis aries*) are living museum pieces in that they are the ancestors of the first sheep domesticated by early Britons. With their fine, swept-back curly horns (the sort invariably shown in depictions of Aries the ram) and dark brown coat, **Soay Sheep** bear little resemblance to the bleating flocks we are used to seeing in fields the length and breadth of the country.

Identifying some common farm sheep

Since the majority of us spend most of our lives away from St Kilda and Lundy, some sort of handle on a few breeds of common domesticated sheep will doubtless come in useful.

Swaledale:
White-bodied mountain sheep with black faces but white noses, ears and eye patches, and impressively curly horns.

Cheviot:
Entirely white hill sheep with no horns and an attractive ruff of wool around their necks.

Romney:
Another horn-free all-white sheep, this one has a woolly quiff on top of its head and is found mainly in south-east England.

Suffolk:
A very common sheep with a long white body, black hornless head and black legs.

Mule:
Another very widespread sheep – a cross between the Blue-faced Leicester and one of a number of hill breeds – with a white body, a mottled brown/white face and no horns.

Non-rigweltered sheep

Note well

Sheep have spent centuries building up a reputation for lacking original thoughts and for slavishly yearning to 'follow like sheep'. Since they appear to have no intention of dimming their ambitions in this area, you should refrain from pretending to be a shepherd while passing through a flock of sheep, because although they will enjoy following you to the edge of the field, your inevitable departure over a stile will only distress them.

EASY NATURE

Just remember this:

Soay Sheep are named after Soay, one of the islands of St Kilda, where they were introduced by Viking settlers more or less a thousand years ago.

- The name Yorkshire folk have for a dead sheep is 'rigweltered' (or often just 'rigged'). 'Rig' comes from the Latin meaning 'stiff', while 'weltered' is an Anglo-Saxon term meaning 'upside-down', which rather tells its own sad story.

What you should say:

'We all like sheep have gone astray, old thing.'

The naming of the Shrew

T he common error made about the Shrew is that it is a rodent. However, as a member of the (now defunct) Insectivora order, it is a closer relative of the Hedgehog (p. 30) than the Vole or Mouse (p. 42). After a shake-up in taxonomic circles, the details of which we shan't concern ourselves with, shrews were accorded their own order – Soricomorpha – which, less than informatively, means 'shrew-like'.

Identification

The thing to remember about shrews is that they possess extraordinary noses seemingly fixed like drill bits onto chubby bodies, thus giving them the appearance of miniature tunnelling machines. Couple this with their tiny eyes, and shrews become unmistakeable as a family. This leaves you the simple task of delineating between the three major species, all of which are found throughout the British mainland.

A Common Shrew

Common Shrew (*Sorex araneus*)

The shrew you are most likely to come across. They live more or less anywhere there is enough food to sustain them.
Body length: 5.5cm to 9cm.
Coat: Dark brown on top, lighter brown sides, off-white under-neath.

Water Shrew (*Neomys fodiens*)

A veritable giant among shrews, the Water Shrew is a good swimmer and invariably makes its home near water.
Body length: 6cm to 9.5cm.
Coat: Black on top, white underneath (occasionally black all over).

A Water Shrew

Pygmy Shrew (*Sorex minutus*)

One of Britain's smallest mammals, pipped only by the Harvest Mouse (p. 42) and the Pipistrelle Bat (p. 18).
Body length: 4cm to 6cm.
Coat: Dark brown on top, off-white underneath.

If you find yourself on the Scilly Isles, Jersey or Sark, keep an eye out for the **Lesser White-toothed Shrew** (*Crocidura suave-olens*), which is about the size of the Common Shrew but with grey fur. Unusually, Scilly Isles-based Lesser White-toothed Shrews have taken to rummaging about for food on the beach. Meanwhile, on the Channel Islands of Guernsey, Alderney and Herm, there lives the **Greater White-toothed Shrew** (*Crocidura russula*), which is exactly the same but some-times a tiny bit bigger (body length 5–8.5cm as opposed to 5–8cm). The two can be told apart only by an expert close examination of their teeth or, more easily, by dint of their location, since there is no overlap between them.

EASY NATURE

Just remember this:

Shrews must munch through roughly their own body weight in insects, worms, slugs and snails every day in order to survive.

• Sadly, the Shrew has nothing to do with the town of Shrewsbury, the name of which is a corruption of the Old English 'Scrobbesbyrig', meaning 'fortified place in the scrubland'.

What you should say:
'I'll pheeze you, in faith.'[1]

---

[1] The opening line of William Shakespeare's *The Taming of the Shrew*.

Whale meat again

The waters off the British Isles are teeming with the sort of exotic sea-life that is usually associated with deep oceans and the distant swaying of palms. Hosts of different *cetaceans* – whales, dolphins and porpoises – lie off our northern and western coasts. Even mammoths such as the 50-tonne Fin Whale (*Balaenoptera physalus*) can occasionally be seen off Scotland. We will content ourselves, however, with a look at those species you might be lucky enough to see without having to go on a specialised boat trip.

Whales

Minke Whale (*Balaenoptera acutorostrata*)

The only whale that regularly invades Britain's inland waters, the Minke (pronounced Minky) can sometimes be seen around the Inner and Outer Hebrides. It has a small but distinctive hook-shaped dorsal fin and a pointed snout.
Length: To 10m.
Colouring: Very dark grey, often appearing black.

Sperm Whale (*Physeter macrocephalus*)

Occasionally, a ferry passing between the Scottish mainland and the Shetland Islands will encounter a Sperm Whale, an enormous mammal weighing up to 40 tonnes. Despite its huge blunt head, it can keep up nearly 30mph for an hour or so if need be. It possesses a dorsal 'hump' rather than a fully-fledged fin.
Length: To 20m.
Colouring: Black, or as near as makes no difference.

Dolphins

Common Dolphin (*Delphinus delphis*)

The world's most numerous cetacean is probably also its best-loved one. Those who have swum with a dolphin often claim to have had a mystical intra-species connection with them. Sadly, thousands of dolphins are still killed each year in Tuna and Sea Bass catches.
Length: To 2.5m.
Colouring: Dark grey upper, off-white undersides.

Bottlenose Dolphin (*Tursiops truncatus*)

Can be seen, on occasion, from the shore of the Moray Firth, which enjoys a particularly benign micro-climate. This dolphin's distinctive nose resembles the top of a bottle, as the name suggests.

Length: 3–4m.

Colouring: Grey-brown, darker on top than underneath.

Porpoises

Harbour Porpoise (*Phocoena phocoena*)

This fastidiously shy and stubby porpoise is often mistaken for a dolphin. Infrequently seen off the north Devon coast, near Lundy, or off the Inner Hebrides.

Length: To 2m.

Colouring: Dark grey on top, off-white underneath.

How to tell the difference between a dolphin and a porpoise

	Dolphin	*Porpoise*
Length	To roughly 4m	To about 2m
Leading edge of dorsal fin	Curved	Straight
Snout	Pointed	Blunt
Voice	Audible	Inaudible to humans
Social community	Large groups	2 to 4 maximum

EASY NATURE

Just remember this:

The **Killer Whale** (*Orcinus orca*) is actually a sort of dolphin.

What you should say:

'Icelanders, Canadians, Alaskans, Grenadans, Dominicans, St Lucians, Faroe Islanders, Greenlanders, Norwegians and Japanese – lovely people and all that, but the blood of many whales and dolphins cries out against them and one day there will be a reckoning.'

Boar to be wild

The ancestor of today's domesticated Pig, Wild Boar (*Sus scrofa*) roamed the forests of Britain long before Caesar set foot in the country. Hunted mercilessly for their meat and skin, the last British Wild Boar was killed sometime in the 17th century. The woodlands of the nation were not to hear their grunts and squeals again until the late 1980s when, ever resourceful, some imported Boar effected a daring escape from a breeding farm and, even more spectacularly, an abattoir. Since then, there has been a rash of bids for freedom (sometimes with a little covert human help) in various parts of the country, resulting in the establishment of a handful of small colonies of the animal.

A Wild Boar

Identification

Often mistaken for Muntjac Deer (p. 25) or escaped farm pigs, the Wild Boar looks essentially like a pig but is dark brown/black, very furry, and considerably slimmer. The male adult has two lower canine teeth that point upwards like tusks.

Where are they?

There are fewer than a thousand Wild Boar in Britain, all of them in England. Although there have been alleged sightings at dozens of locations, the existence of viable communities has been confirmed only in five places. The largest group – estimated to be around 200-strong – is on the **Kent/East Sussex** border near Ashford, close to where the two original escapes occurred. There are also smaller populations living on **Dartmoor**, Devon; near **Bridport**, Dorset; in the **Forest of Dean**, Gloucestershire (one individual was even seen wandering around a Co-op supermarket); and near **Ross-on-Wye**, Herefordshire.

The good and the bad

Although their grazing methods are beneficial in the regeneration of woodland, it has to be admitted that there is a downside to the second coming of the Wild Boar: they can cause damage to crops and even a small group can devastate local populations of ground-nesting birds. Furthermore, there is the danger of them spreading swine fever or foot-and-mouth disease. However, although caution is advised when encountering Wild Boar, they do not pose a great risk to the public, since they are likely to attack only when cornered or if they feel that their young are threatened.

The return of the natives

The Wild Boar's return to the British countryside has been entirely unplanned. However, there are campaigns calling for the deliberate reintroduction of the Wolf (*Canis lupus*), the Lynx (see p. 21), the Walrus (*Odobenus rosmarus*) and the European Brown Bear (*Ursus arctos*), among other animals.

EASY NATURE

Just remember this:
Wild Boar piglets are easily identified by
the long horizontal stripes on their backs.

What you should say:
'At the risk of being a wild bore,
I'm rather glad they're back.'

The much maligned Bindweed

No flower with 'weed' in its name is ever likely to get a fair press. Certainly there are not many gardeners with a kind word to say for bindweed – a very pernicious plant that is liable to take over domestic plots if not dealt with in a robust manner. In the wild, however, bindweed often beautifies ugly spaces such as brownfield sites and the waste-ground next to railways. Natural climbers (save for Sea Bindweed, which prefers to trail over the ground), they are also very distinctive with their 'His Master's Voice' gramophone-horn flowers and heart-shaped leaves.

A problem arises only when it comes to differentiating between the four types of bindweed common to these shores. However, this difficulty is by no means insuperable. In order to work out which species you are dealing with, simply put what you can see through the following tests.

Flower colour	Flower length[1]	Location	Bindweed type
White or pink	Up to 7cm	Hedges, fens, damp woods	Hedge
White or Pink	Up to 9cm	Waste ground, fences, hedges	Large
Pink with five white stripes	Up to 2cm	Farms, verges, hedges	Field
Pink with five white stripes	Up to 5cm	Sandy or shingly beaches	Sea

[1]The length of the bindweed flower is given so that, even if closed (such as at night or in cloudy weather), you can still measure it.

When do they flower?

Sea Bindweed (*Calystegia soldanella*)	June to August
Field Bindweed (*Convolvulus arvensis*)	June to September
Hedge Bindweed (*Calystegia sepium*)	July to September
Large Bindweed (*Calystia sylvatica*)	July to September

EASY NATURE

Just remember this:

As species names go, those of the bindweed couldn't really be any more helpful. The flowers of Large Bindweed are *large*. Hedge Bindweed is often found in a *hedge*. Field Bindweed is usually found in a *field*. Sea Bindweed lives near the *sea*.

*Hedge
Bindweed*

- Field Bindweed is often an ingredient of Noyeau, a liqueur used in cooking.

- Sea Bindweed is also known as Prince's Flower in Scotland (where it is rare). The legend goes that Charles Edward Stuart (Bonnie Prince Charlie) landed on the Isle of Eriskay in 1745 and scattered the plant's seeds there. Sea Bindweed still grows on Eriskay and nowhere else in the Outer Hebrides.

- The root of Field Bindweed is diuretic, laxative and, unsurprisingly, enormously purgative.

What you should say:

'Bindweeds, bindweeds, bindweeds.' (Stroke chin.) 'It's a little-known fact that those that climb always do so anti-clockwise.'

Forage for Borage

Borage's old-fashioned-sounding name turns out to be entirely apt because it has enjoyed an extremely long history of use by humans. The plant traces its origins to ancient Syria and its English name to the Arabic *abu'arak*, which means 'father of sweat', a reference to its value as a diaphoretic. However, helping people sweat out fevers is merely one in a whole myriad of ways in which Borage has been put to use. Over the years it has served as a dye, a herb, a salad leaf, an oil (which is still produced commercially today), a tea, an insect repellent and a medicine for colds, bronchitis and respiratory infections. Nowadays, the edible baby blue flowers of the 'herb of gladness' are also frozen into ice cubes and tossed into sophisticated cocktails. If this were not enough, Borage also has its own family named after it, members of which include Comfrey, Forget-me-nots and the dramatic scarlet Hound's Tongue.

Where to find it

Borage (*Borago officinalis*) chanced upon in the wild in Britain is likely to be an escapee from a garden. Since it is able to survive on very poor soil, it can often be seen colonising rubbish tips and waste ground. You are also likely to have been beaten to it by bees, who find Borage nectar very attractive.

Common Forget-me-not
(*Myosotis arvensis*)

The dainty pastel pink or blue Forget-me-not is one of those flowers that fringed every lawn just a few decades ago but which has fallen from fashion in gardens today. In the wild, try looking for 'Scorpion Grass', as it is sometimes known, at the edges of woods, by roadsides and on sand dunes from April to September.

Common Borage

• The English herbalist John Gerard (1545–1611) claimed that eating Borage leaves brought joy, and that a syrup made from Borage 'purgeth melancholy and quieteth the phrenticke and lunaticke person'.

Common Comfrey (*Symphytum officinale*)

Common Comfrey's clustered droplets of unassuming yellow or purple flowers can be seen near bodies of water from May to September. Like Borage, the latter half of Common Comfrey's Latin name – *officinale* – means that it was once sold as an 'official' medicinal herb, since Comfrey also has multiple curative uses (see p. 227).

Common Comfrey

EASY NATURE

Just remember this:

Borage is also known as 'The Starflower' because its flowers resemble stars (albeit blue ones).

What you should say:

'In Somerset, folk wore Forget-me-nots in May to protect themselves from witches. Not any more though, probably.'

High-energy bulbs

As anyone who has gone for a walk in a wood in springtime will tell you, Daffodils are not the only bulbs. A basic knowledge of the commonest bulbs will give your walking companions the impression that you possess no little expertise in this area. Add a couple of the rarer species to your roster and the illusion is complete.

Common bulbs

Bluebell (*Hyacinthoides non-scripta*)

Identification: Bell-like flowers, actually more violet than blue.

Flowers: April–June.

Nugget to drop: The larger **Spanish Bluebell** (*Hyacinthoides hispanica*) is pushing out the native English variety. It's the Grey Squirrel/Red Squirrel story of the plant world.

Ramsons (*Allium ursinum*)

Identification: Long garlic-smelling leaves and clusters of white star-shaped flowers.

Flowers: April–June.

Nugget to drop: Also known, unsurprisingly, as Wild Garlic, its leaves are very good in salads.

Snowdrop (*Galanthus nivalis*)

Identification: Familiar white nodding flowers.

Flowers: January–March

Nugget to drop: Named after the snow often around when it flowers, rather than the colour of the flowers themselves.

Wild Daffodil (*Narcissus pseudonarcissus*)

Identification: Distinctive yellow horns on stout stems (to about 35cm).

Flowers: Late February–April.

Nugget to drop: Vies with the Leek and the Dragon as the national symbol of Wales.

Wild Daffodils

A couple of more exotic varieties

Winter Aconite (*Eranthis hyemalis*)

Identification: Yellow upward-facing flowers that look like huge
buttercups on short stalks (up to 10cm).

Flowers: January to early March.

Nugget to drop: All parts of the Winter Aconite are poisonous.

Winter Aconite

Snakeshead Fritillary (*Fritillaria meleagris*)

Identification: The flowers have a purple chessboard look and
really do resemble drooping snakes' heads. Grows to about
40cm.

Flowers: April–May.

High-energy bulbs cont.

Nugget to drop: The meadow at Magdalen College, Oxford, is famous for its Snakeshead Fritillaries, which have been growing there in abundance since at least 1785.

EASY NATURE

Just remember this:
To tell the difference between Spanish and English Bluebells, smell them – the English version is heavily scented.

A cautionary note

The Crocus, often thought to be a bulb, actually grows from a *corm*. The *stigma* of *Crocus sativus* is better known as saffron, a spice more expensive, by weight, than gold. Also, the plural form is Crocuses and not Croci, no matter what people with a classical education may tell you.

Two other 'bulbs' that are not bulbs

Although they can often be found flowering in the same places and at the same time as bulbs, Wood Anemones and Lesser Celandine are *not* bulbs. Wood Anemones grow from special roots called *rhizomes*, while Lesser Celandine emerge from *tubers*.

Lesser Celandine

Lesser Celandine

(*Ranunculus ficaria*)

Identification: Bright yellow flowers (eight to twelve petals) on short stalks (to 25cm).

Flowers: January–May.

Nugget to drop:
It provides a welcome early food source for nectar-gathering insects.

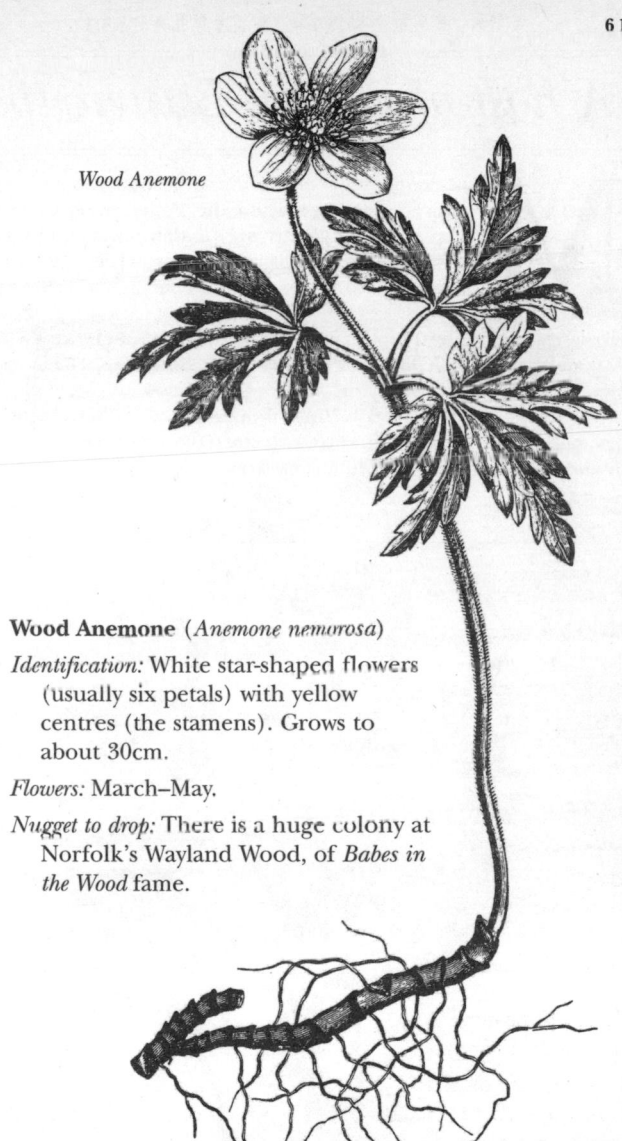

Wood Anemone

Wood Anemone (*Anemone nemorosa*)

Identification: White star-shaped flowers (usually six petals) with yellow centres (the stamens). Grows to about 30cm.

Flowers: March–May.

Nugget to drop: There is a huge colony at Norfolk's Wayland Wood, of *Babes in the Wood* fame.

What you should say:

'The Lesser Celandine's other name, Pilewort, comes from its long use in the successful treatment of piles.'

A host of golden Buttercups

Most people's first encounter with a buttercup occurs at a very tender age when the flower is thrust under their chin by a cheery peer to detect a predisposition towards butter. Since, under normal lighting, there is no reason for any child's chin not to reflect the buttercup's yellow petals, it is safe to say that this does not constitute a failsafe test for lactose intolerance. The buttercups of choice for this dubious trial are the low-growing Creeping Buttercup (*Ranunculus repens*) and Bulbous Buttercup (*Ranunculus bulbosus*), examples of which scatter the country in their hundreds of millions between May and August. However, just as with the daisy family (p. 68), a few minutes' work on the wider buttercup family can reap rich rewards.

Meadow Buttercup

The buttercups that look like a buttercup should:

The **Meadow Buttercup** (*Ranunculus acris*) is basically a Creeping Buttercup on stalks (up to 1m). As the name helpfully suggests, it is often found in meadows (May to September).

Lesser Celandine (*Ranunculus ficaria*) is recognisable by each flower's eight to twelve thrusting yellow petals which give it the look of a child's painting of the sun (p. 60). Seek them out in deciduous woodlands and boggy meadows (January to May).

Marsh Marigolds (*Caltha palustris*) have buttercup-like flowers with furry centres and glossy kidney-shaped leaves, and are usually found near water (March to July).

Members of the buttercup family that really don't:

It is with these that you will most be able to impress those around you with your knowledge of the arcane workings of the Linnaean system of classification (see pp. 208–11).

Traveller's Joy is a happier name for **Old Man's Beard**, in that travellers coming across the great champagne-bubble explosion that is a bush of *Clematis vitalba* in full bloom cannot but feel delight at the sight (July to August).

The **Wood Anemone**'s (*Anemone nemorosa*) six-pointed white stars are among the most spectacular of spring flowers (p. 61) that adorn the floor of Britain's woodlands (March to May).

EASY NATURE

Just remember this:

Old Man's Beard is so called because its fruits are white and feathery, like an old man's beard.

- In 'Spring Offensive', First World War poet Wilfred Owen tells of buttercups that 'had blessed with gold' the boots of soldiers on their way to the front and probable death.

- The Bulbous Buttercup (*Ranunculus bulbosus*) is also known as Crowfoot, Goldcup, Frogsfoot and St Anthony's Turnip.

- In *Love's Labours Lost*, Shakespeare refers to buttercups as the 'Cuckow buds of yellow hew'.

What you should say:

'Why, look! The cuckow buds of yellow hew, as the Bard once put it. *Love's Labours Lost*, if I recall correctly.'

The difficulty with Carrots

No one should expect plaudits for correctly identifying a carrot. The missile-shaped root crop has been, after all, part of the staple diet of Britons since the reign of Elizabeth I. However, the carrot's undomesticated relatives are another matter altogether. Not only are three of them – Hemlock, Cowbane and Fool's Parsley – poisonous, but there are also over a dozen common wild carrots that, from a distance, appear all but indistinguishable.

Identification

The key to sorting one wild carrot species from another is not to panic, for each one is endowed with one or two distinguishing features. Commit these to memory and all of a sudden the carrots begin to look less like peas in a pod and more like the rugged individuals they are.

Name	Height	Flowering	Distinguishing Feature/s
Alexanders	To 1.5m	Apr–June	Yellowy-green flowers/almost always near coast
Burnet-saxifrage	To 0.5m	July–Aug	Upper and lower leaves entirely different
Cow Parsley	To 1.5m	Apr–June	Hollow stems/lace-like flowers
Cowbane	To 1.5m	July–Aug	Flat stems and seeds/favours reed beds
Fool's Parsley	To 1.3m	July–Aug	Pointed green bracts hang from umbels
Ground Elder	To 1m	May–July	Leaves divided into three leaflets
Hemlock	To 2m	June–July	Nasty smell/purple-blotched stems
Hogweed	To 2m	June–Sept	Deeply notched petals of outer flowers
Rock Samphire	To 0.5m	July–Oct	Yellow flowers on rocky coastlines
Rough Chervil	To 1m	June–July	Purple-spotted hairy stems
Sweet Cicely	To 1m	May–June	Smells like aniseed
Wild Angelica	To 2m	July–Sept	Pinkish flowers
Wild Carrot	To 1m	July–Aug	Red or purple flower in centre of umbel

Carrot Glossary

Most carrots
produce umbrellas
of flowers called
umbels. The *bracts*
that distinguish Fool's
Parsley (*Aethusa cynapium*)
from Cow Parsley (*Anthriscus
sylvestris*) are nothing more
exotic than modified leaves.

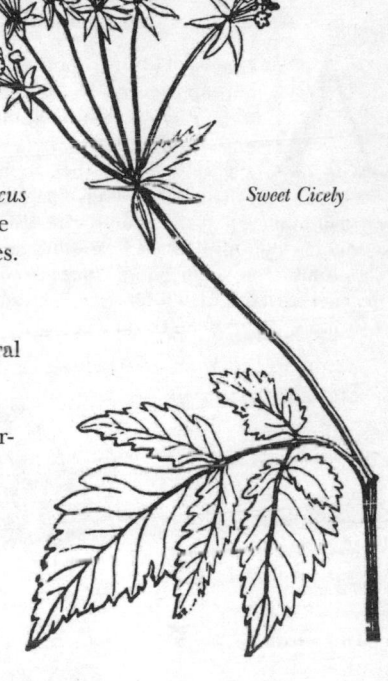

Sweet Cicely

What you should know

Near the sea, the ever-plural
Alexanders (*Smyrnium
olusatrum*) takes over from
Cow Parsley, which is otherwise southern England's
commonest carrot; and
Burnet-saxifrage
(*Pimpinella saxifraga*) is so
called because it looks
like a plant called Salad
Burnet and grows
among stones (Latin
sax) but sadly is not related to Burnet or Saxifrage.

EASY NATURE

Just remember this:

Cowbane (*Cicuta virosa*) is so called
because it is the bane of cows (and indeed
is poisonous to all grazing animals).

What you should say:

'The reason the Athenian authorities forced
Socrates to drink a fatal cup of Hemlock was
because he shone a light on their evil deeds.'

Cranesbills, hard but fair

AOne of the great joys of familiarising yourself with the unprepossessing **Herb Robert** is that once you've done so, you'll begin to see it more or less everywhere. Indeed, unless you're in the far north of Scotland, it's difficult to get away from the seemingly delicate but actually extremely tenacious little flower. This hardiness masked by an appearance of frailty is a quality shared with other members of the family, such as the cheeky **Dove's Foot Cranesbill** and the will-o'-the-wisp **Meadow Cranesbill**. The family name comes from the fact that once their flowers have died off, what is left (the *calyx* and *pistil*) looks like the head of a Crane (a bird similar to the Heron).

Coming to grips with the Cranesbills:

Step 1 – Herb Robert
Herb Robert (*Geranium robertianum*) owes its nicknames 'Stinking Robert' and 'Stinky Bob' to its rather upsetting mouse-like odour. Don't let this put you off, however, for you have to get pretty close to it to pick up its rodenty scent, and it makes up for it with very becoming pink flowers, each with five petals, and blood-red stems that sprawl along the ground, rarely getting higher than 50cm. Look out for it in shady places

Herb Robert

such as woods, hedgerows, bank sides and forgotten corners of gardens. It flowers from May to September.

Step 2 – Dove's Foot Cranesbill

Similar to Herb Robert, Dove's Foot Cranesbill (*Geranium molle*) has slightly smaller flowers (about 1cm) than its relative and leaves that do not bear such an alarming resemblance to Victorian wallpaper designs. More striking still, each of its flowers' five petals end in unmistakeable mouse-ears (like the aptly named **Field Mouse-ear** – p. 91). If you have a particularly good imagination, you might be able to see the leaves as somehow reminiscent of the feet of doves, but otherwise the nomenclature is not altogether helpful.

Step 3 – Meadow Cranesbill

Although blessed with the intricate leaves and five-petal flowers of the Cranesbill family, the large violet blooms (to 4cm) of the Meadow Cranesbill (*Geranium pratense*) set it apart from its creeping cousins. Indeed, the flower can grow as high as 1m and between June and September is a common sight in meadows, as its name suggests.

Meadow Cranesbill

EASY NATURE

Just remember this:

Only the hapless and wretched make the error of calling a Cranesbill a 'Cranebill'. You know rather better.

• Herb Robert is the favourite flower of mischievous house goblin Robin Goodfellow (since you ask, Robin is a diminutive of Robert).

What you should say:

'The leaves of Herb Robert, once crushed and rubbed on the skin, are said to repel Mosquitoes.'

Daisy, Daisy

The chances are you can identify the Common Daisy without troubling the further-flung recesses of your brain. What you may not realise is that, with a minimum of application, you can identify other members of the daisy family and so add greatly to your store of accumulated nature know-how.

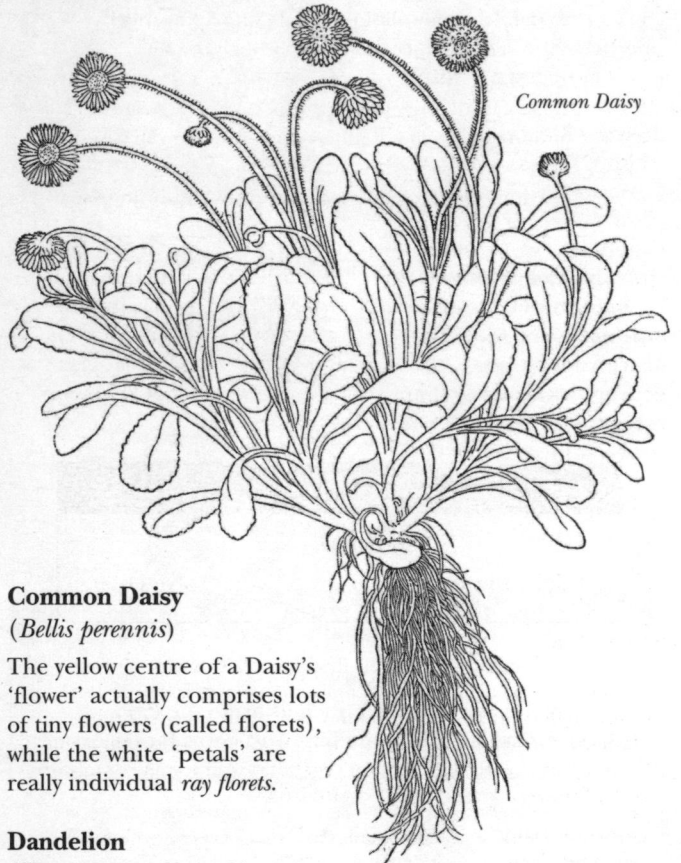

Common Daisy

Common Daisy
(*Bellis perennis*)

The yellow centre of a Daisy's 'flower' actually comprises lots of tiny flowers (called florets), while the white 'petals' are really individual *ray florets*.

Dandelion
(*Taraxacum officinale*)

Growing in almost every lawn in the land, the poor Dandelion is perhaps the most easily recognised but least loved of wild flowers (see p. 70).

Oxeye Daisy (*Leucanthemum vulgare*)

The Oxeye Daisy resembles the Common Daisy but is much larger (flower heads up to 6cm across) and taller (up to 1m). It is not to be confused with **Corn Chamomile** (*Anthemis arvensis*), another daisy, which has smaller flower heads (up to 3cm across) and a rather pleasing scent.

The art of the daisy chain

1. Pick a Common Daisy.
2. Make a narrow slit in the stalk with a fingernail.
3. Thread a second Daisy through the slit.
4. Make a slit in the stalk of the second Daisy.
5. Thread a third Daisy through the slit of the second one.
6. Continue until you have the length of chain you desire.
7. Join up the two end Daisies.
8. Present the Daisy chain to some individual worthy of it.

Other notable daisies include the scruffy but widespread **Hemp Agrimony** (*Eupatorium cannabinum*) which can grow up to 1.5m high – look for large clusters of pinky-white flowers near rivers, streams and lakes; and **Coltsfoot** (*Tussilago farfara*), whose golden flower heads look like Common Daisies crossed with Dandelions.

EASY NATURE

Just remember this:
A daisy the size of an ox's eye is an Oxeye Daisy.

- 'Daisy Bell' (better known by its first line 'Daisy, Daisy, give me your answer do') was composed by Englishman Harry Dacre in 1892. Confusingly, the Daisy in question was actually Frances Evelyn Maynard, the Countess of Warwick – a women's rights campaigner, Labour Party candidate, militant vegetarian and sometime mistress of the Prince of Wales (later Edward VII).

- The word 'Daisy' is derived from 'day's eye' because it closes at night and opens its 'eye' again at dawn.

What you should say:
'I can't afford a carriage. Is there a bus?'

Flowers that look
like Dandelions

The Dandelion is one of nature's successes. Despite the millions of gardeners who attack it on a regular basis with lawnmowers, hoes, poisons and even, ill-advisedly, strimmers, the Dandelion remains one of Britain's commonest plants, an instantly recognisable drop of golden sun on lawns and roadsides from Cornwall to Shetland. Less happily, there is a whole swathe of the daisy family (see p. 71) that mimics the appearance of the Dandelion, and although they are unlikely to be mistaken for it, may quite possibly be mistaken for each other. Some care, therefore, is needed to sort the Hawk's-beards from the Hawkweeds.

Dandelion

Dandelion (*Taraxacum officinale*)
The name of the Dandelion is derived from the French 'dent de lion', meaning 'lion's tooth' (a reference to the plant's serrated leaves). The plant can be used as a diuretic, a coffee substitute, a tea, to make wine, or to treat skin diseases and rheumatism.

Goat's-beard

The look-alikes:

Goat's-beard (*Tragopogon pratensis*)
What to look for: Grass-like leaves.
Height: to 70cm.

Smooth Hawk's-beard (*Crepis capillaris*)
What to look for: Numerous small
    flowers (to 1cm) on thin stems.
Height: to 75cm (though very often
    smaller).

Rough Hawk's-beard (*Crepis biennis*)
What to look for: Much larger flowers
    (to 3.5cm) and hairy stems.
Height: to 1m.

Cat's Ear (*Hypochoeris radicata*)
What to look for: Probably the most
    similar to the Dandelion but
    rather taller (Dandelions rarely
    grow to more than 30cm).
Height: to 50cm.

Autumn Hawkbit
(*Leontodon autumnalis*)
What to look for: Similar to Cat's
    Ear but has smaller flowers (1–3cm)
    that are reddish underneath.
Height: to 50cm.

Common Hawkweed
(*Hieracium vulgatum*)
What to look for: Each stem bears
    several flowers and its leaves are
    oval and jagged.
Height: to 1m.

Mouse-ear Hawkweed
(*Pilosella officinarum*)
What to look for: A single flower (striped
    red underneath) on each stem and
    elongated hairy mouse-ears for
    leaves.
Height: to 25cm.

Autumn Hawkbit

Flowers that look like Dandelions cont.

Smooth Sow-thistle

Smooth Sow-thistle
(*Sonchus oleraceus*)
What to look for: The buds appear more like those of a thistle, while the stem and leaves contain a milky fluid.
Height: to 1.5m.

Field Sow-thistle
(*Sonchus arvensis*)
What to look for: As the Smooth Sow-thistle but with yellow hair on the stems.
Height: to 1.5m.

Bristly or Prickly Oxtongue
(*Picris echioides*)
What to look for: Bristles on both the stems and long narrow leaves.
Height: to 80cm.

Bristly Oxtongue

EASY NATURE

Just remember this:
Goat's-beard is also called Jack-go-to-bed-at-noon because its flowers open only in the morning sun.

What you should say:
'And my childish wave of pity, seeing children carrying down / Sheaves of drooping Dandelions to the courts of Kentish Town.'[1]

---

[1] John Betjeman, 'Pot Pourri from a Surrey Garden'.

Figworts express

The Figwort family is large (around 3,000 species) and curious, being an odd mixture of tall robust plants such as the **Foxglove** and **Great Mullein** (which can grow to over 2m) and tiny creepers such as **Common Field Speedwell** (p. 96). More perplexing still, the family's scientific name is Scrophulariaceae, which is hard enough to pronounce, let alone remember. However, since so many flowers are Scrophulariaceae, an ability to spell the word marks out the serious naturalist from the mere dabbler.

> **What you should remember about the Scrophulariaceae**
>
> i. Most of them bear flowers on vertical spikes.
> ii. They usually have quite regulated leaves – either opposite or alternate.
> iii. Their flowers often have four or five petals.

Four of the main players

The **Foxglove** (*Digitalis purpurea*) is an easily identifiable plant with its big floppy leaves and up to 80 tubular purple flowers hanging off a tall spike (up to 1.5m). They're a common sight almost every-where but the fens of East Anglia and some parts of south-east England where the soil is too chalky for them.

Great Mullein

Taller still, with huge oval leaves but less spectacular flowers, is the **Great Mullein** (*Verbascum thapsus*). Also called Aaron's Rod, because its spike thrusts up to the heavens like a staff, its tiny yellow flowers look much like sweetcorn kernels on a cob. The plant is used by herbalists in the treatment of asthma.

More modestly proportioned (up to about 80cm) is the **Common Toadflax** (*Linaria vulgaris*). However, it more than makes up for its relative lack of stature with its two-tone yellow flowers (up to 3cm) that have a very distinctive outline, like a parrot sitting on a perch.

As you might expect from a plant with ivy-shaped leaves, the **Ivy-leaved Toadflax** (*Cymbalaria muralis*) likes to climb walls and sprawl about in a rather louche fashion. Look out for its purple stems and lilac-and-yellow flowers, which are similar in form but about half the size of those of the Common Toadflax.

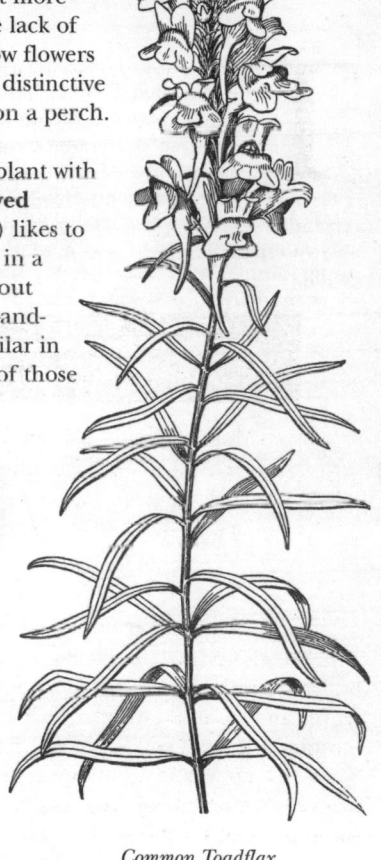

Common Toadflax

Three things you should know about the Foxglove

i. Its Latin name means 'purple fingered'.

ii. It likes nothing more than a bit of disturbed soil in which to grow.

iii. It's poisonous, so if anyone offers you Foxglove crumble, just say no.

EASY NATURE

Just remember this:

The flowers of Foxgloves could just about be used as gloves by a Fox, but he'd have to be quite an emaciated one.

What you should say:

'Scrophulariaceae – that's three a's, two e's, one p.'

Heather, the goddess of Scotland

T he definitive Scottish poet Robert Burns is the greatest champion heather has ever had. In his verses, he (or some lassie) is forever straying 'amang the heather' on the way to or from trysts with lovers in byres. There is a good reason why they might be doing this: Scotland comes alive with heather from July to September, and the purple hue with which it carpets the heaths and moorlands is a perfect backdrop to any number of romantic assignations. Happily for amorous Britons living south of the border, heather is not confined to Scotland but can be seen wherever acid soils prevail.

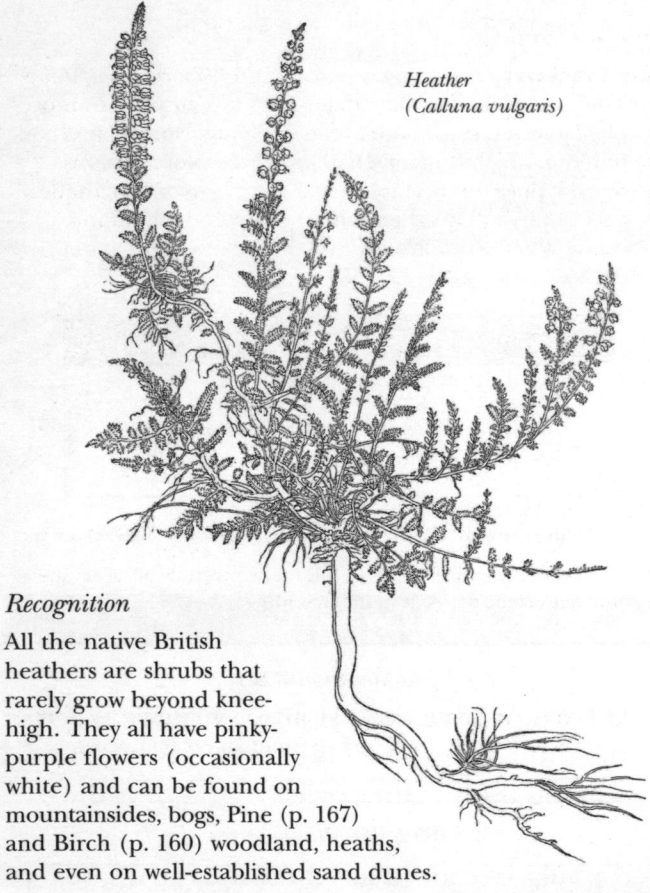

Heather
(*Calluna vulgaris*)

Recognition

All the native British heathers are shrubs that rarely grow beyond knee-high. They all have pinky-purple flowers (occasionally white) and can be found on mountainsides, bogs, Pine (p. 167) and Birch (p. 160) woodland, heaths, and even on well-established sand dunes.

Five heathers that seem like heathers

The most common heather is not called Common Heather or Moorland Heather, as one might expect, but simply **Heather** (*Calluna vulgaris*). Its stems are woody, while its purple flowers are small (to 0.5cm) but plentiful. **Bell Heather** (*Erica cinerea*) appears similar from a distance but has leaves like pine needles and bell-shaped flowers (to 0.6cm). **Cross-leaved Heath** (*Erica tetralix*) has larger flowers (to 0.9cm) that are pink and the shape of rugby balls. **Dorset Heath** (*Erica ciliaris*) is found only in Dorset, Cornwall and Dartmoor, and bears reddish-purple flowers that are more elongated (to 1.2cm). **Cornish Heath** (*Erica vagans*) grows only on the Lizard peninsula in Cornwall, and has small mauve or pink flowers.

Two heathers that do not

Both **Cranberry** (*Vaccinium oxycoccus*) and **Bilberry** (*Vaccinium myrtillus*) are heathers, a fact that comes as a surprise to most people. However, since both are low creeping shrubs and both are found in much the same habitats as the more obvious heathers, it does not require such a great leap of imagination to think of them as heathers, and it behoves the budding naturalist to get over his or her initial astonishment as swiftly as possible.

EASY NATURE

Just remember this:

To differentiate Heather from all the other heathers, refer to it by its other name: Ling.

- Heather ale is known to have been made by Picts over 3,000 years ago.

- White heather is said to be lucky, but this is probably because one is fortunate to come across it in the first place.

What you should say:

'At barn or byre thou shalt na drudge, / Or naething else to trouble thee; / But stray amang the heather-bells, / And tent the waving corn wi' me.'[1]

---

[1] Robert Burns, 'Bonie Jean'.

The ineffable pinkness of Mallows

One of the many joys of the mallow family is that one of its members is actually called a **Marsh Mallow**. Better still, it turns out that the plant was the original source of marshmallow, the gungy confection that adds such a charming pink-and-white scum to the surface of otherwise perfectly good hot chocolate. Sweet manufacturers have long since dispensed with Marsh Mallow as an ingredient, and so it is left to its own devices along with its many relatives, including **Common Mallow** and **Tree Mallow**, both of which are found in abundance in Britain.

Common Mallow (*Malva sylvestris*) can be seen almost anywhere in England, but is rarer in Wales and Scotland. Its unmistakable large flowers (up to 4cm) with their five purple-veined shocking pink petals brighten up roadsides, waste ground and other unloved or untended crannies. Growing up to 1.2m in height, Common Mallow can also be seen waving at passing trains from June to September.

Common Mallow

Tree Mallow (*Lavatera arborea*)
The flowers of the Tree Mallow share the same colours and number of petals as the Common Mallow, though the centres of the former are rather darker. Both mallows also have large leaves that resemble hands with webbed fingers, albeit fingers that have been bitten around the edges. However, instead of the widely separated petals that make the Common Mallow so distinctive, the Tree Mallow sports flowers with overlapping petals that form large cups (up to 5cm).

Marsh Mallow
(*Althaea officinalis*)
There can no mixing up
the Marsh Mallow with its
two confederates because
its leaves are almost trian-
gular and its five-petalled
flowers (up to 5cm) are a
very much more delicate
shade of pink, the sort
that, if it were a shower
gel, would doubtless be
called 'touch of satin' or
'spring rain'. Although
the Marsh Mallow (up to
1.5m) is apt to grow
higher than the Common
Mallow, it still manages to
appear much less robust.
Look for it near streams
and brackish ditches,
around the edges of salt
marshes and in coastal
areas.

Marsh Mallow

EASY NATURE

Just remember this:

If you see a mallow that is between 2 and 3 metres in
height, like a small tree, you can be sure it is a Tree Mallow.

- Common Mallow leaves make an excellent addition to salads.

- Tortoises are very partial to the flowers of Tree Mallows but turn up
  their noses at the leaves.

- Extract of Marsh Mallow can be used to treat ulcers.

What you should say:

'It is indeed no coincidence that the flowers
of the Marsh Mallow are a colour somewhere
between a pink marshmallow and a white one.'

Minty fresh

The mint family not only provides us with mints to suck and flavourings for the toothpaste employed afterwards, but also a wide range of herbs including one, **Oregano**, without which Italian dishes are scarcely worth the name. Add **Wild Basil** and **Wild Thyme** into the mix and the mints suddenly become one of our most gastronomically important families. It is therefore a pity that the mint that springs first to mind – Spearmint (*Mentha spicata*) – is not a native of these shores but of Central and Southern Europe.

Corn Mint and Water Mint

The cartoon drawing of the mint leaf that habitually appears on Spearmint-flavoured products is usually a good starting point for identifying **Corn Mint** (*Mentha arvensis*) and **Water Mint** (*Mentha aquatica*): serrated oval leaves, similar to the Nettle (p. 82), and small pale pink flowers lumped together in bunches on the stem at the base of each leaf. Water Mint grows the higher (to about 90cm rather than 60cm) and smells very strongly of mint, whereas Corn Mint has a fainter, more peppery aroma.

Water Mint

Marjoram

Better known in the kitchen as Oregano, **Marjoram** (*Origanum vulgare*) has similar-looking flowers to the Corn and Water Mints, but with smaller oval leaves. Naturally, a sure test is to rub a leaf to check whether it smells of Oregano, although it should be kept in mind that dried Oregano often has a more pungent aroma than its fresh form.

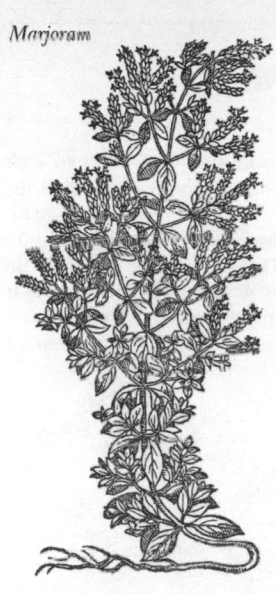
Marjoram

Wild Basil

Unlike Basil grown for the pot, Wild Basil (*Clinopodium vulgare*) is only very slightly scented. This means that to identify it you will look out for a mint-like plant but with darker pink flowers and leaves the shape of spearheads running up the stems. Unlike Corn or Water Mint, Wild Basil favours dry ground such as open woodland and grassy banks.

Wild Thyme

A plant that spreads along the ground and bears little resemblance to what one might suppose a Mint to look like, aside from its pink flowers that grow in the familiar over-populated heads. The leaves of Wild Thyme (*Thymus polytrichus* or *Thymus praecox*) are very much smaller (to 0.8cm), and can form something of a mat on the ground once the plant has become established.

For your further consideration

Other members of the mint family include the **Dead-nettles** (p. 83), the rectangular-leaved **Wild Sage** (*Salvia nemorosa*) and the white-flowered **Gypsywort** (*Lycopus europaeus*).

EASY NATURE

Just remember this:

Water Mint is the mint that grows by *watery* places
(streams, rivers, lakes, marshes etc.).

What you should say:

'The Gypsywort is clearly a remnant of
an age less politically correct than our
own – almost no one today believes that
the Roma people dye their skin with it.'

Nettled

A plant with an unhappy reputation, the Common Nettle (*Urtica dioica*) is actually one of Britain's most important native species. Without the humble nettle we would lose some of our best-known butterflies, like the Red Admiral and Small Tortoiseshell (both pp. 106–7), whose larvae feed exclusively on its leaves. A large nettle can also produce up to 40,000 seeds, thus providing a banquet for seed-eating birds.

The when and where of the nettle

When seen: All year round.

Where seen: Abundant throughout Britain.

Home: Will grow on almost any soil. Favours sunny spots.

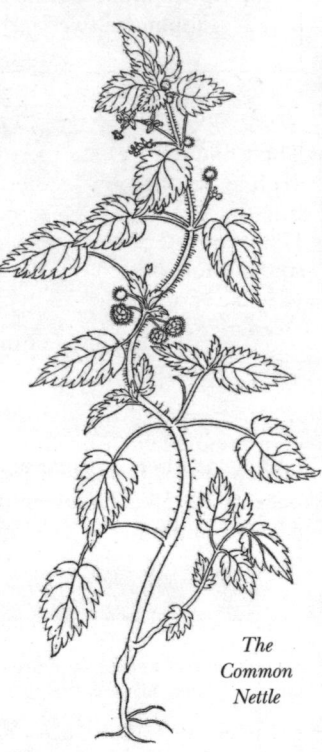

The Common Nettle

Recognition

- Grows in clumps up to 2m high.
- Dark green square stems.
- Leaves that look like the edge of a saw.
- Covered with tiny hairs.
- If you are above 820m, the plant you are looking at is *not* a nettle.

EASY NATURE

Just remember this:
Nettles lose their sting if they are chopped, crushed or cooked.

Nettle soup
(a source of iron, calcium and magnesium)

i. Cook with a knob of butter for ten minutes.

ii. Mash resultant pulp.

iii. Add garlic, cornflour, milk and seasoning.

iv. Serve piping hot to anyone who'll have it.

Top tip: To avoid serving Gritty Nettle Soup, pick only the topmost leaves and never harvest after June.

Tricks with nettles

The Common Nettle's hairs break at the slightest touch and act like hypodermic needles, injecting a cocktail of poisons into the skin, including serotonin, histamine and formic acid. However, you can amaze onlookers by plunging your hands into a whole bush of nettles without being stung. The trick is to make sure the nettles in question are the stingless **White Dead-nettles** (*Lamium album*) or **Red Dead-nettles** (*Lamium purpureum*). These look exactly the same as the Common Nettle, but have white or pink flowers near the top.

If you mistakenly attempt this trick with stinging nettles, gain instant relief by rubbing the affected skin with a leaf from a nearby **Broad-leaf Dock** (*Rumex obtusifolius*). This works because the alkaline juices in the dock leaf neutralise the acids from the nettle. Top tip: dock leaves don't work for wasp stings, which are also alkaline.

• The Bottle Inn in Dorset holds an annual nettle-eating competition.

• The stems of nettles were used by our ancestors to make cloth and ropes.

• National 'Be Nice to Nettles Week' takes place each year in May.

• Cornish yarg is hand-wrapped in nettle leaves, which apparently helps the cheese to ripen.

What you should say:
'If only you understood the nettle, you would love it as I do.'

Nightshade,
the poisoner's friend

There can be few plants as evocatively named as the night-shades, and there's something satisfyingly grim about Britain's three common variants: **Woody Nightshade**, **Black Nightshade** and **Deadly Nightshade**. Troublingly, they come from the same family (Solanaceae) as potatoes, tomatoes and peppers. It goes without saying, of course, that no part of any of the nightshades should be tasted, even if it seems like a good idea at the time.

Woody Nightshade

Woody Nightshade or **Bittersweet** (*Solanum dulcamara*) is a climber with tomato-like leaves that is found in hedges or near water. From June to September look for its striking star-shaped lilac flowers, each with a yellow stamen sticking out like a tiny straightened banana. It produces mildly poisonous green berries which ripen to a bright red.

Woody Nightshade

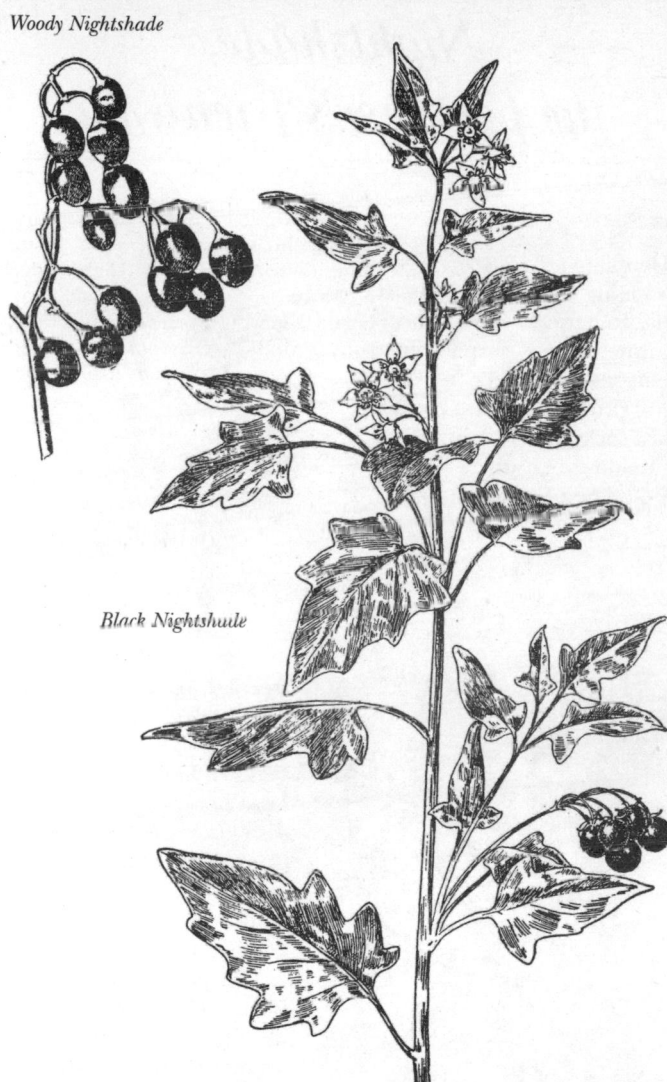

Black Nightshade

Black Nightshade (*Solanum nigrum*) resembles the potato plant and has white rather than lilac flowers (though it shares the same tell-tale 'banana' stamens with Woody Nightshade). Its berries become less poisonous as they turn from green to black.

Nightshade,
the poisoner's friend cont.

Henbane (*Hyoscyamus niger*) is a highly toxic nightshade. It has tomato-like leaves and funnel-shaped purple-veined pale yellow flowers, but does not produce berries. Henbane is a sticky, hairy plant with a noxious smell which keeps would-be predators at bay.

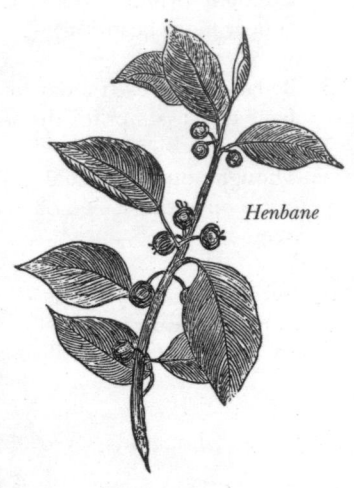

Henbane

Deadly Nightshade

Deadly Nightshade (*Atropa belladonna*) is the source of belladona and one of the Western hemisphere's most poisonous plants. Also known as Sorcerer's Cherry, Witches' Berry and Murderer's Berry among numerous other cautionary monikers, Deadly Nightshade has unremarkable oval leaves, muddy purple bell-shaped flowers and red berries that ripen to black. However, the berries are not as poisonous as the leaves (a single one can kill an adult), which are, in turn, less toxic than the roots.

What you should know about belladonna

i. The substance (which means 'pretty lady') probably got its name from women of the Spanish court who used to drink a diluted form in order to dilate their pupils (and thus appear more beautiful).

ii. Belladonna is used today by optometrists to achieve the same effect (if not for the same ends).

iii. Though potentially fatal to humans, belladonna has no effect on a wide range of animals, including birds and deer.

iv. Bill Wilson, a co-founder of Alcoholics Anonymous, is said to have taken a course of belladonna in an unsuccessful attempt to wean himself off alcohol.

v. The poison visits upon its victims a sense of timelessness and a feeling that they are flying.

EASY NATURE

Just remember this:
Atropa belladona is the name given to Deadly Nightshade because *belladona* contains the poison *atropine*.

What you should say:

'An innocent enough looking plant, Deadly Nightshade, but during the Parthian Wars it is said to have wiped out much of the army of Marcus Antonius.'

The wonder of Peas

J
ust as with the carrot family (p. 64), it is a blunder of the first order to imagine that the peas resemble the vegetable plant that graces the nation's dinner plates. When thinking about peas, novice naturalists are much better served by connecting them with grassland, for that is where the majority are found. For example, no lawn or meadow is complete without its smudges of clover, the commonest pea within our shores; while, on closer inspection, the yellow fringes of silky cliff-edge greenswards are often found to be Kidney Vetch, a seaside pea.

The Clovers

So common that it is routinely dismissed as a weed, clover can form a spectacular summer carpet of red or white, and is also an important source of food for many butterflies. The **White Clover** (*Trifolium repens*) is easily identified by its familiar leaves, formed of three leaflets, and white spherical flower heads. The **Red Clover** (*Trifolium pratense*) is not just an aberrant White Clover but a distinct species. When not in flower, look for off-white semi-circular markings on the leaves. Red Clover can be used to treat respiratory disorders.

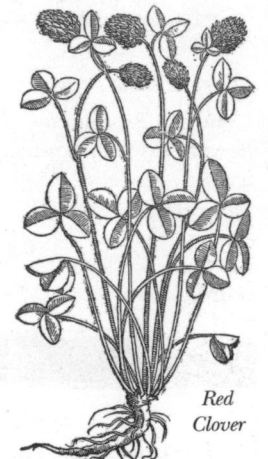

Red Clover

The Vetches

Their purple Pea-like flowers and long spikes with pairs of narrow leaflets running up them make Vetches very distinctive. Differentiating the **Common Vetch** (*Vicia sativa*), **Bush Vetch** (*Vicia sepium*) and **Tufted Vetch** (*Vicia cracca*) is easy. The first is hairy, the second virtually hairless, while the third produces a plethora of flowers (up to 40 per spike). Their coastal cousin, **Kidney Vetch** (*Anthyllis vulneraria*), more often sports yellow flowers in tight clusters. All bloom throughout the summer.

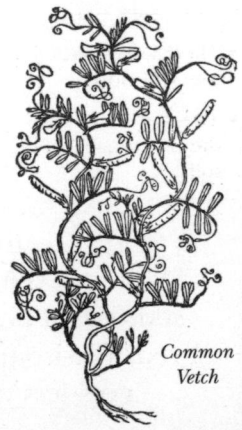

Common Vetch

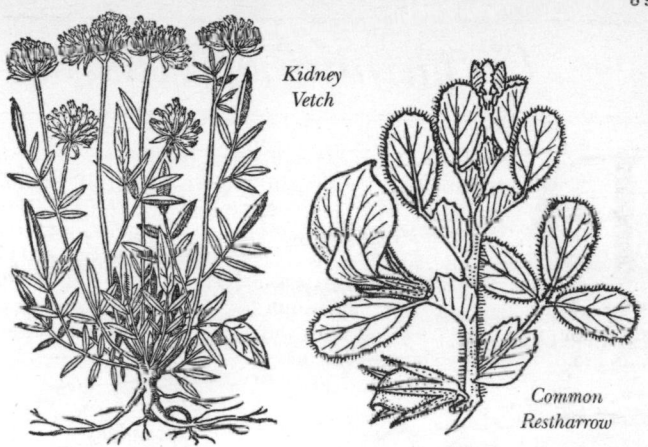

Kidney
Vetch

Common
Restharrow

Other notable Peas

Common Restharrow (*Ononis repens*) has relatively large pink flowers (to 2cm) and stubby leaves comprising one or three leaflets. The cheery yellow flowers of **Bird's-foot Trefoil** (*Lotus corniculatus*) look rather like a balloon twister's attempts at making cartoon arrow symbols. **Sainfoin** (*Onobrychis viciifolia*) has beautiful slim flower heads composed of small purple-veined white flowers that resemble raspberry ripple ice cream.

EASY NATURE

Just remember this:

The Latin name for clover – *Trifolium* – simply means three-leaved. *Tres* = three; *folium* = leaf. Folium gives us the word *foliage*.

- There are estimated to be around 10,000 three-leaf clovers for every four-leaf clover.

- The Restharrows are so called because their stems are so strong that they are capable of stopping harrows (a tool used for loosening top soil).

What you should say:

'The four leaflets of the four-leaf clover stand for Faith, Hope, Love – the three great Christian virtues – and Luck, which gets less of a look-in, biblically. '

Think Pinks

Domesticated members of the pink family (also known as the carnation family but more scientifically as the Caryophyllaceae) have long been a staple in British gardens. In the wild, one of the most important genera[1] of the pink family is the campion. Being both numerous and widespread, campions rather force themselves upon the attentions of would-be naturalists who, with a little care, will swiftly add four species to their growing list of recognisable wild flowers.

White Campion

Four common campions

With flowers about 2.5cm wide that are actually more of a pink colour, the **Red Campion** (*Silene dioica*) grows to around 75cm and is often seen on roadside verges and the edges of woods. The West Country of England in particular is a sea of pink from May to July.

[1]This is the plural of genus, and well worth the noting.

Similar looking and almost as common, the **White Campion** (*Silene alba*) has white flowers (about 3cm wide), grows to about 1m, and favours hedgerows and rough patches in lowland areas (flowers May to September).

So called because of its large 'bladder' (actually a *calyx*) at the base of each flower, the **Bladder Campion** (*Silene vulgaris*) blooms from June to August, is more widespread than the White Campion, and enjoys the same habitats.

At first sight, the **Sea Campion** (*Silene maritima*) might be mistaken for the Bladder Campion. However, while the latter grows to about 1m, the Sea Campion spreads itself about in cushions, rarely growing higher than 25cm. Its leaves are smaller, its flowers slightly bigger (up to 2.5cm across), and it is found almost exclusively near the seashore.

Other pink family members of note

(All the following have white petals.)
Field Mouse-ear (*Cerastium arvense*), with its petals that end in mouse ears; the rather dowdier **Common Mouse-ear** (*Cerastium fontanum*); the five petals of the **Greater Stitchwort** (*Stellaria holostea*) notched to look like ten; and the seemingly ubiquitous tiny-flowered **Common Chickweed** (*Stellaria media*).

EASY NATURE

Just remember this:

The vast majority of pinks are not pink at all. Indeed, the white family would be a rather more fitting name.

- In the same way that the term orange comes from the colour of oranges, the name to describe the colour pink is believed to have come from the flower pink.

- Rather confusingly, Sea Pink (p. 94) has pink in its name and is pink but is not a pink (it's a Sea Lavender).

- The Sea Campion has two scientific names: *Silene maritima* (because it lives on the coast) and *Silene uniflora* (because it produces single flowers).

What you should say:
'A Stitchwort in time saves nine.'

The Primrose family, not like Roses at all

Primroses (*Primula vulgaris*) are as much a part of spring in Britain as Daffodils and new-born lambs. Indeed, the pale yellow flowers with orange hearts can begin appearing as early as December and so are often around to welcome their vernal companions. Adorning almost every corner of the country, the Primrose is a flower that aspiring naturalists would do well to pin down very early on.

What you should know

There are three curious things about the Primrose that mark it out for special attention:

i.   Ants (p. 100) play an important part in its pollination. The insects' thin bodies are perfect for reaching down the long flower tube to get at the nectar at the bottom. In doing so, they unwittingly deliver pollen that has attached itself to their bodies from previous Primrose visits.

ii. It has two types of flower – the orange centres are either 'pin-eyed' (like a five-pointed star) or 'thrum-eyed' (circular). Both sorts of flower need to be present for seeds to be produced.

iii. It was used as a cure for paralysis in the past.

Primrose

The Primrose also gives its name to a whole family of flowers, one member of which is the equally lovely **Cowslip** (*Primula veris*) which blooms in April and May. A hardy perennial that enjoys sunny well-drained meadows, its yellow flowers are smaller than those of the Primrose and much higher off the ground (up to 30cm). Cowslips sometimes cross with Primroses to produce hybrid plants that produce clumps of large flowers riding on tall stalks.

Cowslip

For future study

Other members of the
primrose family include
Chickweed Wintergreen
(*Trientalis europaea*), **Sea
Milkwort** (*Glaux maritima*),
Creeping Jenny (*Lysimachia
nummularia*) and **Scarlet
Pimpernel** (*Anagallis arvensis*), a sweet little thing with
scarlet flowers (though it
sometimes has pink blooms
and very occasionally blue
ones) comprising five round
petals. If you feel the need
to seek them here and seek
them there, Scarlet
Pimpernels can usually be
found flowering near cultivated land or on sand dunes
between June and August.

EASY NATURE

Just remember this:

The name Cowslip comes from the Old English *cuslyppe,*
which means 'cow dung' (Cowslips flourish among cowpats).

- The Scarlet Pimpernel is also called the Shepherd's Weatherglass (a
weather glass being a water-based barometer invented in the 17th
century). This is because its flowers close up when the weather is
about to turn bad, thus alerting any passing shepherds who might
otherwise have been oblivious to the torrential rain soaking them
and their beleaguered flock to the skin.

- Cowslips are called 'Peggles' (or 'Paigles') in certain parts of East
Anglia.

What you should say:

'Them's Peggles, them's are, or my
name's not Ebenezer Gildersleeves.'

Seaside flowers

I t is good to remember that the coast of Britain is home not only
to a range of sea creatures and crustaceans but also to a rich
array of plant life. Since a relaxing holiday by the sea is often the
occasion chosen by those not in the know to ask those whom
they consider knowledgeable about such things to hold forth on
whatever flora might be encountered therein, it is wise to familiarise
yourself with at least a handful of the flowers that enjoy a good sea
breeze.

On the cliff-tops

Thrift (*Armeria maritima*) is the
ubiquitous plant that looks like
chives with lumps of pink bubble-
gum. The flowers (to about 1cm,
April–October) are usually
around 20–30cm off the ground
and supported by leafless
spindly stalks that grow from
a pillow of long narrow
leaves. Also known as Sea
Thrift and Sea Pink.

Thrift

Common Gorse (*Ulex europaeus*) is not solely a coastal phenom-
enon, but there is so much of it around the coast that it is as
well to know what it is. It is an evergreen shrub that delights
in snagging the jumpers of passing walkers. It grows to about
2m and produces a plethora of golden-yellow flowers (all year
round, but more so in spring) that can often be seen from a
great distance. What is less well known is that those flowers
have a smell rather like coconuts.

Other common cliff-top dwellers dealt with elsewhere include
Kidney Vetch (p. 88) and **Sea Campion** (p. 91).

By the shore

Biting Stonecrop (*Sedum acre*) looks something like a cactus
with its fleshy stems and spiky flowers – five-petal bright yellow
stars (about 1.2cm). Since it blooms only in June and July,
concentrate on acquainting yourself with the plant's stems:
imagine a tall pile of bowls arranged by a waiter on his first
day in the job.

Common Sea-lavender
(*Limonium vulgare*) is a
flower that lives up to its
name. It is common, it
lives by the sea and it has
lavender-like flowers (lines
of purple along tall stems,
July–October). Better still,
you can tell at once that it
is not lavender because it
has large, thick oval leaves
at its base.

Common Scurvygrass
(*Cochlearia officinalis*) is so
called because it contains
Vitamin C and so was fed
to sailors to prevent scurvy.
It is another cactus-like
plant with small heart-
shaped leaves and very
distinctive flowers
(May–August) comprising
four white (sometimes
pink) 'teeth' growing from
a green centre.

Common Sea-lavender

EASY NATURE

Just remember this:
Biting Stonecrop is also called Wall-pepper
because it is often found growing on walls
and its leaves have a peppery taste.

What you should say:
'When Gorse is out of bloom,
kissing's out of season.'[1]

---

[1] Old folk saying.

All's well that's Speedwell

I f you spy a clump of dainty blue flowers in a meadow, a culti-vated field or by a hedge in spring or summer, there's a good chance you're looking at one of the speedwells. In fact, unless you're sure the flowers are some other species, such as Harebells or Forget-me-nots (p. 56), assume that they probably are some sort of speedwell until you have checked all their alibis. Unfortunately, the picture is complicated by the fact that some common speedwells are not blue but purple, mauve or lilac. However, once you have begun to become familiar with the various blue speedwells' flowers, recognition of their violet-hued cousins should become second nature.

Recognising the speedwells

There are hundreds of species of speedwell throughout the world, so it's best to start by master-ing a handful and moving outwards from there.

Common Field Speedwell
(*Veronica persica*)

A.k.a.: Persian Speedwell, Large Field Speedwell and Bird's Eye.

Identification: A sprawling plant with sky-blue veined flowers (about 1cm) and small jagged leaves.

Flowers: All year.

Where: Cultivated fields (where farmers regard it, not surprisingly, as a weed).

Common Field Speedwell

Germander Speedwell (*Veronica chamaedrys*)

Identification: Similar to Common Field Speedwell but taller (to about 25cm) with deeper blue flowers and larger, almost nettle-like, leaves.

Flowers: March to July.

Where: Meadows, hedgerows and deciduous woodland.

Heath Speedwell (*Veronica officinalis*)

A.k.a.: Paul's Betony

Identification: Although the plant has the speedwellesque flowers, they are smaller (about 8mm), lilac and there are around twenty of them to a stem (about 15cm).

Flowers: April to August.

Where: Woodland, heaths, moors and pasture.

Ivy-leaved Speedwell (*Veronica hederifolia*)

Identification: Another straggler with very small but very hairy leaves that make it look almost like a cactus. Flowers (5mm) are light blue with dark veins and white centres.

Flowers: March to August.

Where: Cultivated fields and brownfield sites.

For future study

Thyme-leaved Speedwell (*Veronica serpyllifolia*): light blue flowers with dark veins (8mm). **Wall Speedwell** (*Veronica arvensis*): minute blue flowers (3mm). **Brooklime** (*Veronica beccabunga*): clusters of blue flowers (7mm). **Slender Speedwell** (*Veronica filiformis*): copious lilac-blue flowers (8–10mm).

EASY NATURE

Just remember this:

All speedwells are from the Veronica genus, so you can be absolutely sure of getting at least their first name right.

- Common Field Speedwell seems very much at home in Britain, but it arrived from Asia as recently as the 1820s.

- The green parts of Heath Speedwell have been used for centuries in the treatment of coughs and gastric ailments. It was once also used as a substitute for tea, though not a very pleasant one.

What you should say:

'The fleshy leaves of the Brooklime make a refreshing alternative to watercress.'

Willowherbs,
the indefinite flowers

Willowherbs are precisely the sort of plants you see in a bit of scrub while on a walk that cause you to reflect: 'I'll never be able to name them, no matter how long I study nature – they're just not anything enough.' This may, perhaps, be close to the truth when they are not in flower but, come the summer, there is no excuse for not being able to pin down these elegant flowers, no matter that they appear too typically wild-flower-like at first glance.

Pinning down the willowherbs

Start with the easiest one, **Rose-bay Willowherb** (*Chamaenerion angustifolium*), which sports tall spikes of purply-pink flowers (each one about 3cm) between May and September, and reaches a height of around 1.3m. Its leaves are nothing to get too excited about, being long and thin and fairly nondescript, but it should be remembered that even a lack of striking features can help the observant naturalist. For instance, should you see a plant with similar purply-pink flowers but *exotic looking* leaves, you know you can eliminate Rose-bay Willowherb from your enquiries.

Rose-bay Willowherb

Move on next to **Great Willowherb** (*Epilobium hirsutum*), the tallest member of the family (to 1.5m) but one lacking the exuberant flowers of the Rose-bay, with which it shares similar leaves. This means you will have to imagine what the Rose-bay would look like if it were slightly taller, had individual purply-pink flowers (about 2cm) instead of whole spikes of them, and very hairy stems.

Once you have mastered these two, you can graduate to the trickiest of the common Willowherbs – **Broad-leaved Willowherb** (*Epilobium montanum*). Humble in stature (to 60cm), with small flowers (1cm) a slightly paler pink, and leaves a similar shape to those of the Rose-bay (if slightly broader), the Broad-leaved Willowherb can often go unremarked. Your mission, should you choose to accept it, is to track it down – it is plentiful enough in Britain, flowers all summer, and inhabits a wide range of locales including woods, hedgerows and even stone walls, so in theory it shouldn't be an impossible task.

In time, you may even find yourself confident enough to stow one of the family's exotic members up your sleeve, such as **Enchanter's Nightshade** (*Circaea lutetiana*), with its tiny white flowers (June to August) and fat shiny leaves.

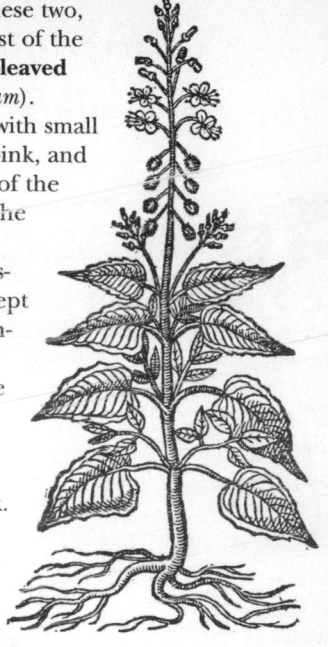

Enchanter's Nightshade

EASY NATURE

Just remember this:

Even after the summer, it is still possible to recognise the willowherbs by their long thin pods which burst to release oodles of fluffy white seeds.

What you should say:

'*Chamaenerion angustifolium* … it's impossible not to draw the conclusion that sometimes that Mr Linnaeus was having a laugh.'

No time for antics –
the driven world of the Ant

Ants have been known as the workaholics of the insect world since long before the writer of the Book of Proverbs scolded: 'Go to the ant, thou sluggard; consider her ways and be wise.' Her ways is indeed the correct form, since most male ants ('drones') are dead within a few weeks, leaving the work to the females, which is perhaps how it should be.

The life of an ant

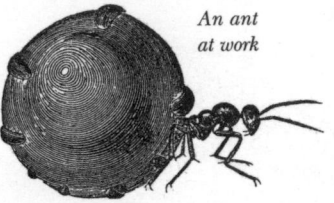

An ant
at work

A fertilised ant egg becomes a female; an unfertilised one, a male; and both pass through larval and pupal stages on their way to adulthood. Males are born exclusively to breed. They spend their short lives eating before flying off to mate on the wing with fertile females, who then break their own wings off and form new colonies. The sterile female ('worker') is back at home looking after the queen, and feeding and moving the larvae and pupae. She is soon promoted to making improvements to the colony's home, and finally to defending the nest or foraging outside it, the two most dangerous tasks. Meanwhile, the colony's queen (or queens, in the case of some species) shoulders the difficult task of government.

Some common British ants

Black Garden Ant (*Lasius niger*)

Try to train yourself to refrain from using the term 'black ants', since this is a somewhat loose description that could be readily applied to dozens of different species in Britain alone. The Black Garden Ant is the most commonly encountered 'domestic' ant, particularly as it is a species that tends to search far and wide for food for the colony.

Red Ants (*Myrmica rubra* and *Myrmica ruginodus*)

Fairly frequent visitors to gardens, these two species of Red Ant (a term you can use with impunity) are often more the colour of stem ginger than a true red. They can sting humans (and anything else) without thereby committing suicide. *Myrmica rubra* is the only ant of any sort on the Orkney Isles.

Southern Wood Ant
(*Formica rufa*)
Also known as the Horse Ant, the reddish Southern Wood Ant lives in woods in the south of England. Their connection with horses is less well established, but they are Britain's largest native species (to 1cm) and, like many of the better developed ants, can spray formic acid at their foes.

Southern Wood Ant

EASY NATURE

Just remember this:
The British county purported to have the most ant species is Dorset, with 33.

- Ants are found everywhere in the world except Hawaii, Iceland, Greenland and Antarctica.

- Worker ants may survive for three years, while queens may live to be 30.

- Ants are estimated to make up around 20 per cent of the world's animal biomass.

- Many birds such as Starlings (p. 142) and Crows (p. 114) practise 'anting' – rubbing ants against their feathers to release formic acid, a powerful insecticide and fungicide.

- Ants actively farm aphids for the honeydew they excrete.

What you should say:

'Don't trr-ead on an ant, he's done
nothing to you. / There might come a
day when he's treading on you.'[1]

---

[1] 'Antmusic' (Ant, Pirroni).

Things that buzz

Bees, wasps and hornets – all members of the Hymenoptera order, which also includes ants (p. 100) – are often labelled respectively as 'the good guys', 'the bad guys', and 'the guys about whom we don't really know much aside from the fact that they hover'. However, this is only one third true. While bees generally *are* a good thing, wasps do their bit in reducing the aphid population, and if you see a hornet hover, you're probably looking at a Hover Fly (p. 110).

The bees

Aside from supplying honey – the **European Bee** (*Apis mellifera*) being the apiarists' work-horse of choice – bees do sterling work pollinating plants. As is well known, the European Bee dies after stinging its foe, but the 200+ species of the friendly **Bumble Bee** (whose genus is *Bombus*) can sting repeatedly with impunity. However, the honour of being the third insect to have its entire genome mapped fell to the European Bee, which must be some consolation.

European Bee

The wasps

The **Common Wasp** (*Vespula vulgaris*) and **German Wasp** (*Vespula germanica*) look almost exactly the same, but you can appear brilliant by identifying the latter by the three tiny black dots on its face. Both are social wasps, and build paper nests from chewed wood and saliva.

An unpleasant thought

Tiny parasitic wasps typically inject their eggs into the bodies of hosts who are then eaten alive from the inside (the vital organs being the last parts to be devoured) as the eggs develop into larvae.

March of the Killer Bees

Killer Bees (or Africanised Bees) are a hybrid of the European and African honey bees, as developed by one Warwick Estevam Kerr in Brazil. A number of queens were accidentally released from his hives in 1957 and they have now made it as far as the southern United States. Although often more aggressive than European Bees, the danger they pose to humans has been laughably hyped by the world's media.

European Hornet

The hornet

European Hornet
(*Vespa crabro*)
Slightly larger than its close relative the Common Wasp, the European Hornet is far less aggressive. It can be identified by the reddy-brown thorax above the familiar 'wasp-like' yellow-and-black abdomen. There is no truth in the popular warning that three hornet stings can kill a human, although several hundred might.

EASY NATURE

Just remember this:

The oft-quoted 'fact' that physicists have worked out that, given its wing-surface and beats-per-second-to-weight ratio, the Bumble Bee should not be able to fly, is an urban myth.

• Honey bees do a 'waggle dance' for their hive mates to let them know, with astonishing accuracy, the direction and distance to particularly good sources of nectar, pollen or water.

What you should say:

'Kill a hornet in Germany and you face a possible 50,000 euro fine. Now that's a civilised people and no mistake.'

Beetlemania

The order of Coleoptera (lit. 'sheathed wing') – beetles to you and me – has more species (370,000) in it than any other order in the animal kingdom. It is thus not incumbent upon you to name all known beetles, or even half of them, but a stab at a handful of families shouldn't be beyond you.

Woodworm (Anobiidae family)

The places where woodworm have been are more often seen than the woodworm themselves. However, listen out on summer evenings and you might hear the mating call of the **Death Watch Beetle** (*Xestobium rufovillosum*), a tapping or a faint scratching sound. Seeing one is meant to presage death, although not necessarily the viewer's. The **Common Furniture Beetle** (*Anobium punctatum*) is a brown-and-black-striped innocuous-looking thing, never more than 0.5cm long, but its seeming ubiquity has made it synonymous with the term 'woodworm'.

Number of species: 1,500

Stag Beetles

Stag Beetles (Lucanidae family)

Britain's largest land beetle is the **Stag Beetle** (*Lucanus cervus*), and the huge antleresque mandibles of the male make it arguably its most fearsome. Now found only in southern

England and in danger of disappearing altogether as its natural habitat – old and dead trees – are cleared away by over-zealous forest managers.

Number of species: 1,300

Fireflies (Lampyridae family)

Identification in Britain is simple because there are just two native species, the **Common Glow Worm** (*Lampyris noctiluca*) and the **Lesser Glow Worm** (*Phosphaenus hemipterus*), of which the latter is very rare. Thus, if you see a small insect in some crepuscular wood using bioluminescence to produce a light with a wavelength between 510 and 670 nanometres, you can put good money on it being the Common Glow Worm.

Number of species: 2,000

Ladybirds (Coccinellidae family)

Whatever your school friends might have told you in the play-ground, the number of spots on a ladybird does not, sadly, have any correlation with its age. Rather, a ladybird with a spot on each half of its shell is likely to be the **Two-spot Ladybird** (*Adalia bipunctata*), and then it's just a question of counting the dots to identify such as the **Seven-spot Ladybird** (*Coccinella septempunctata*), the **Ten-spot Ladybird** (*Adalia decempunctata*), and even the **Twenty-two-spot Ladybird** (*Psyllobora vigintiduo-punctata*), among many others. Of course it's not quite as simple as this, since a lot of spotted ladybirds have names unrelated to their spots, while others are of the [insert number here]-spot variety yet have markings that have morphed beyond all recognition. However, as a starting point you could do worse.

Number of species: 5,000

EASY NATURE

Just remember this:

Roughly one out of every three insects in the world is a beetle.

What you should say:

'The Russian for ladybird is Bozhya Karovka, or "God's Cow". Odd lot, the Russians.'

The Butterfly flutters by

In the world of the butterfly, it is always wiser for the beginner not to bite off more than he or she can chew. Therefore, before you migrate onto the **White-letter Hairstreak** (*Satyrium w-album*) or a stray **Ripart's Anomalous Blue** (*Polyommatus ripartii*), it's as well to nail down first those butterflies you are more likely to come across in a common or garden garden (or common) rather than on some cliff-side fastness or lonely moor.

Life-cycle

Begin your foray into the butterfly's domain by acquainting yourself with the rudimentaries of its life-cycle:

i.   Egg (usually laid on a leaf).
ii.   Caterpillar (feeds on the plant before excreting a silk that forms a case around itself).
iii. Pupa or chrysalis stage (don't say 'cocoon' – it will only show you up).
iv.   Butterfly (you know it's about to emerge when the pupa becomes transparent).
v.   Male and female butterflies mate.
vi.   Female lays egg.

Identification

Since one British butterfly often looks much like another in terms of its size and shape, their identification relies on a knowledge of the colours and patterns on their wings. The good news is that many common butterflies have very distinctive features that make them easily recognisable with a modicum of effort.

Peacock (*Nymphalis io*)

Look for: Markings that mimic those of a Peacock, particularly the 'eyes' which this butterfly uses to scare off predators.

Where: Gardens, meadows and hedgerows.

When flying: July–September.

Red Admiral (*Vanessa atalanta*)

Look for: Two bands of red around a sea of chocolate brown.

Where: Wherever flowers grow (particularly Buddleia).

When flying: May–October.

Large White (*Pieris brassicae*)

Look for: A single dark dot on the
forewing.

Where: Farmland, gardens and
meadows.

When flying: April–October.

A Peacock

Small Tortoiseshell
(*Nymphalis urticae*)

Look for: Orange fringed with
yellow and black up front and
neon blue behind.

Where: Fields, gardens, verges, meadows.

When flying: March–October.

Three myths about the Cabbage White

i. *It's called a Cabbage White.*
Not really. Its proper name is the rather more prosaic Large
White. There is also a **Small White** (*Pieris rapae*) which is
similar but smaller, and a **Cabbage Moth** (*Mamestra brassicae*)
which is a completely different kettle of fish.

ii. *Its larvae eat only cabbage.*
Not so. They are just as happy devouring other brassicas such
as cauliflowers or mustard.

iii. *It lives for just a single day.*
Not at all. They actually flit around for a few weeks on average.

EASY NATURE

Just remember this:
The White-letter Hairstreak has a white
streak in the shape of the letter W.

What you should say:

'Don't go too close! A butterfly fluttering its
wings here can change the weather in Moscow.'

The Dragonfly and the Damselfly

Not quite the Holy Grail of the novice naturalist – but often adjudged to be on a par with discovering the lost city of Atlantis – is the ability to tell the difference between dragonflies and damselflies. Both are wont to flit along lazy summer streams, both come in a dazzling variety of colours and both have absurdly long, thin bodies (or, more properly, abdomens). If this were not bad enough, damselflies technically *are* dragonflies since the dragonfly order (Odonata) is split into two sub-orders: Dragonflies (Anisoptera) and Damselflies (Zygoptera). Thankfully, there are some simple rules to apply to prise the two apart. After that, there just remains the task of deciding what sort of dragonfly or damselfly you are looking at.

How to tell the difference between a dragonfly and a damselfly

The damselfly rests with its wings above it or slightly open.
The dragonfly rests with its wings horizontal or pointing slightly downward.

The damselfly's hindwing is much the same as its forewing.
The dragonfly's hindwing is wider its base than is the forewing.

The damselfly is a relatively sedate flyer.
The dragonfly is one of the quickest insects on the planet.

Any 'damselfly' with a wingspan over 6cm is a dragonfly.

The damselfly's eyes are separated.
The dragonfly's eyes are so close that they touch.[1]

[1]With one British exception: the Club-tailed Dragonfly (*Gomphus vulgatissimus*).

Britain's three commonest dragonflies

Common Hawker (*Aeshna juncea*)
Male: black abdomen with blue and yellow spots.
Female: brown abdomen with yellow or blue spots.

Common Darter (*Sympetrum striolatum*)
Male: Liverpool FC-red abdomen.
Female: yellow thorax, orange eyes and abdomen.

Four-spotted Chaser (*Libellula quadrimaculata*)
Both sexes: light brown abdomen becoming dark brown
at tip.

Britain's three commonest damselflies

Common Blue Damselfly (*Enallagma cyathigerum*)
Male: sky-blue with black bands on abdomen, same colours in
stripes on thorax.
Female: similar markings but can be green, brown or blue.

Blue-tailed Damselfly (*Ischnura elegans*)
Sexes similar: Mainly black body with one sky-blue band
almost at the tip of its abdomen.

Large Red Damselfly (*Pyrrhosoma nymphula*)
Sexes similar: Red abdomen with narrow black bands.

EASY NATURE

Just remember this:
During their years as larvae, dragonflies
and damselflies consume huge numbers of
Mosquito larvae, which cannot be a bad thing.

- Britain plays host to 34 species of dragonfly and 21 species of damselfly.

- In 1900, a giant swarm of Four-spotted Chasers turned the sky over Antwerp black.

- **Mayflies** are smaller insects altogether, and have only a tiny set of hindwings or none at all.

- Dragonfly Week, run by the British Dragonfly Society, is held annually in mid-June.

What you should say:
'Quick, that one there! No, there. No, there.
Were its eyes touching, did you see?'

No Flies on them (unless they're mating)

Members of the Diptera order have six legs and two wings (or none at all) and many spread diseases to humans and animals. They may be, on the whole, an unpleasant branch of the Insecta class, but the dedicated naturalist puts such considerations aside for the sake of Science.

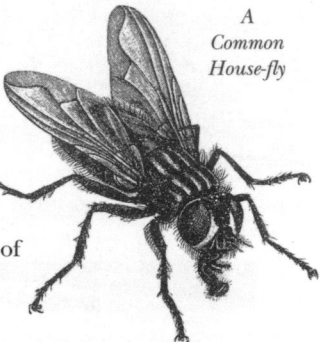

A Common House-fly

Bothersome flies
Common House-fly
(*Musca domestica*)
What good can come of an insect whose eggs are often laid in excrement? The Common House-fly is the stock small black fly with red eyes and a hint of orange at the base of its wings.

Blow Fly
(Calliphoridae family)
An extremely common family of flies – slightly larger than the House Fly, and more bulbous. They have a bristly thorax and dark brown eyes, though not the sort you'd care to lose yourself in.

Attractive flies
Hover Fly
(Syrphidae family)
An easy one – they look like small wasps, feed on the pollen and nectar of flowers, and, as the name suggests, they hover.

EASY NATURE

Just remember this:
Bluebottles are just blue Blow Flies, and **Greenbottles** are green Blow Flies.

Crane Fly (Tipulidae family)
Their slender bodies, paddle-like wings and absurdly extended legs make Crane Flies, or Daddy-Long-Legs, instantly recognisable. They have an endearing if short-lived habit of plunging into the flames of candles.

Painful flies

Mosquito (Culicidae family)
Tiny flies that spread diseases such as malaria, dengue fever,
encephalitis and yellow fever, among others. Thankfully, in
Britain, the worst it can do is give its victims a few days of irri-
tation, the result of the anti-coagulants the Mosquito injects in
order to draw out blood. After a Mosquito has fed, the unwit-
ting donor's blood is clearly visible inside the insect's semi-
transparent body.

Biting Midge (Ceratopogonidae family)
The curse of the Highlands of Scotland, Biting Midges are not
much to look at – a pair of aphid-like wings on a tiny dark
grey body – but they can be very irritating customers. Their
non-biting cousins, the **Non-biting Midges** (Chironomidae
family), look confusingly like Mosquitoes.

Horse Fly (Tabanidae family)
Deliverer of an extremely painful bite, since they slice into the
skin with their mandibles rather than administering a
Mosquitoesque injection. Horse Flies (or Gad Flies) are large,
jet black and, as with the Biting Midges, only the females bite
(the males do not have the requisite mouthparts, but no
doubt they would bite too if they could).

**How to avoid getting bitten by the Biting Midge
if you have forgotten the anti-midge cream**

* Wear white or light-coloured clothing.
* Stay out in the sun.
* Keep on the move.
* Avoid sitting outside in the early morning or late evening.
* Get into a breeze.
* Go indoors (midges rarely enter buildings, even those
  with windows and doors wide open).
* Eat some Marmite every day for a fortnight before
  entering a midge region.
* Avoid the Biting Midge season (June to August).

• It is estimated that malaria, which is spread by Mosquitoes, kills a
human being every twelve seconds.

What you should say:

'For reasons as yet unknown, Mosquitoes have
a preference for the blood of children, which is
probably the best thing about being an adult.'

I can't believe they're not Butterflies

Pity the moth. Unloved on account of its fondness for holing clothes, and widely viewed as the dowdy cousin of the butterfly, it is no surprise that there has been little outcry at the fact that two-thirds of British moth species have been in decline since the late 1960s and that 62 actually became extinct in the country in the last century.

It is perhaps time that we reappraised the lowly creature. For starters, only a very few moth species in Britain actually feed on textiles – the **Common** (or **Webbing**) **Clothes Moth** (*Tineola bisselliella*), the **Case-Bearing Clothes Moth** (*Tinea pellionella*) and the **Brown House Moth** (*Hofmannophila pseudospretella*) being the usual culprits. Furthermore, although a lot of moths may lack the eye-catching brilliance of butterflies, many make up for it in subtle markings that are overlooked by all but close observers. And if this were not enough, millions of moths make the ultimate sacrifice every year, being eaten by birds and bats whose own existence is dependent on them.

Emperor Moth

For the novice naturalist, moths have another thing to recommend them – they are really pretty easy to distinguish from butterflies:

i.   In flight – butterflies are more active during the day, whereas most moth species prefer to fly at night. Moths are also famously attracted to light, like moths to a flame.

ii. At rest – butterflies fold their wings together. With a few notable exceptions, such as the **Bordered White** (*Bupalus piniaria*), most moths tend to lay theirs out like a tent unless particularly uneasy about the presence of possible predators.

iii. Flight season – unlike summer-loving butterflies, there are moths on the wing in Britain all year round.

Know your moths from your behemoths

Emperor Moth (*Saturnia pavonia* or *Pavonia pavonia*)
Its distinctive double set of 'eyes' can often be observed during the day in April or May.

Six-Spot Burnet (*Zygaena filipendulae*) and **Five-Spot Burnet** (*Zygaena trifolii*)
With six and five red spots respectively on startling metallic green forewings that appear black at first sight, and red hindwings. A daytime flier in July and August.

Death's Head Hawk-moth (*Acherontia atropos*)
The largest Hawk-moth in Europe with a wingspan of up to 13cm. Look for the unmistakable skull-like markings on the thorax (the section between the head and the abdomen). Recent mild winters have made it a welcome visitor to southern Britain.

*Death's Head
Hawk-Moth*

EASY NATURE

Just remember this:
There are about 70 species of butterfly in Britain but around 2,500 species of moth.

What you should say:
'If there's no such thing as climate change, why are so many moths moving north?'

Two's company, one's a Crow

There is an old saw that claims: 'If you see one Rook, it's a Crow; if you see lots of Crows, they're Rooks.' This would be a very useful saying indeed if it were not for the fact that it is not always true. However, it can be said that Rooks are more sociable types, while Crows prefer a more solitary existence. This is why we can speak of the existence of Rookeries but not Croweries. Rather more confusing is that Crows are merely one member of the larger crow family (Corvidae) that also includes Rooks, Jackdaws, Ravens, Choughs, Magpies and Jays, among others. Thus, if you point at a Rook and declare it a Crow, you are still technically correct. Should you wish to be a little more precise in your pronouncements, however, you might want to observe the following simple guidelines:

Hooded Crow (*Corvus corone corvix*)

Easily identified by grey markings on its body that make its black head look like a hood.

A Hooded Crow

Carrion Crow
(*Corvus corone corone*)

Often heard before it is seen on account of its raucous 'caw'. The Carrion Crow will happily live up to its name by tucking into dead sheep or roadkill. Watch for it flicking its closed wings when perched.

A Carrion Crow

Rook (*Corvus frugilegus*)

While the Carrion Crow has black feathers under its bill, the Rook has a bare patch of skin there which makes it look as though it's wearing a balaclava.

Jackdaw
(*Corvus monedula*)

Has a very noticeable black crown on its head and calls 'Jack' (but sadly not 'daw').

A Jackdaw

Red-Billed Chough (*Pyrrhocorax pyrrhocorax*)

You should feel very chuffed if you see one, because there are only around 300 pairs in Britain, mainly in Wales, western Scotland, and Cornwall, where they have just been reintroduced. Slightly smaller than Crows, and with red bills.

Raven
(*Corvus corax*)

By far the largest of the Crows, the Raven has a huge beak and is found only in the west of Britain.

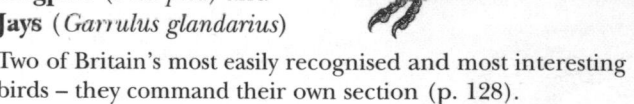

A Raven

Magpies (*Pica pica*) and Jays (*Garrulus glandarius*)

Two of Britain's most easily recognised and most interesting birds – they command their own section (p. 128).

- As is well known, should the Ravens abandon the Tower of London, the kingdom of England will fall. Currently keeping Albion from disaster are Gwylum, Thor, Hugine, Munin, Branwen, Bran, Gunulf and Baldrick (their wings have been clipped, just to be on the safe side).

- Ancient Celts looked upon Crows as sacred and fed them the severed heads of enemies killed in battle.

- Unlike humans, Crows can see the ultraviolet range of the spectrum.

What you should say:

'King Arthur is said to have become a Chough after he died. Or perhaps a Raven, no one's quite sure.'

The multi-coloured world of the Duck

It is a common error to imagine that Mallards are the alpha and omega of the duck world. In reality, the duck family is a large one and roves far beyond the parochial pond in the park. They are wildfowl – a designation that also includes geese, swans and Shelducks (a bird somewhere between a duck and a goose) – and as such have webbed feet (and are consequently good swimmers). From an identification standpoint, ducks are very good news because they all have a similar 'duck' shape which even small children latch on to very speedily. Furthermore, many of them have distinguishing features or colouring that makes recognition a relatively simple task, particularly when compared with other bird families.

Some ducks

Eider (*Somateria mollissima*)

A sea duck with a mighty 'door stop' bill. Males are black and white in winter (mainly black in summer), females an undistinguished but well camouflaged muddy brown. *Length:* 60cm. *Where:* Mainly Scottish coasts.

A Mallard

Mallard (*Anas platyrhynchos*)

The green-headed drake is the archetypal 'duck'; while the female is clothed in more demure shades of brown, a camouflage to protect her from predators such as Foxes when she is sitting on the nest. Mallards can live to the ripe old age of 25. *Length:* 60cm. *Where:* Everywhere.

Pochard (*Aythya ferina*)
The drake has a wonderful chestnut head (in spring) with a grey body and black wingtips; the female and summer male have light brown heads.
Length: 45cm. *Where:* Widespread, only coastal in Scotland.

Shelduck (*Tadorna tadorna*)
A handsome duck with a pronounced red bill, with a precise patchwork of black, white and chestnut, and a dab of green on the wings.
Length: 60cm. *Where:* Widespread but almost entirely coastal.

Shoveler (*Anas clypeata*)
Similar in markings to the Mallard, but smaller and with a huge, black unmistakable 'shovel-like' bill.
Length: 50 cm. *Where:* Most of England, southern Scotland and Anglesey.

Teal (*Anas crecca*)
Britain's smallest duck, the female is a mottled grey/brown, while the drake has an intricate black-and-white body, like the fine designs on bank notes, and a brown head with a distinctive green eye-patch.
Length: 35cm. *Where:* Widespread.

Tufted Duck
(*Aythya fuligula*)
The tuft on the back of the head is more noticeable on the drake, who is black with a patch of white on the body. Female similar but brown.
Length: 45cm. *Where:* Widespread.

> **EASY NATURE**
>
> *Just remember this:*
> Traditional eiderdowns are filled with down from the breast of the female Eider.

Wigeon (*Anas penelope*)
In winter, the drake is another chestnut-headed duck (though with a yellow forehead) with a grey, white and brown body. In summer, both duck and drake opt for muted browns. Look for their short black-tipped grey bills.
Length: 50cm. *Where:* Widespread, particularly in winter.

What you should say:
'Give me Wigeons over Pigeons any day.'

A *pinch* of Finch

There is no getting around it, finches are fat. This is evidently an impediment for a creature that must take to the air to survive, but the brave finch gets around it by using furious bursts of energy. This involves a spurt of desperate fast flaps followed by a closed-wing swoop followed by a bout of swift flapping again to attain some more height. This method of flight is endearing to the onlooker but very energy-intensive, so finches are constantly on the look-out for food and are only too happy to frequent bird tables.

The self-evident finches

Bullfinch (*Pyrrhula pyrrhula*)
The Bullfinch wears a black hood above its pink-red chest (or beige chest, in the case of females) and as such looks only like itself.

Chaffinch (*Fringilla coelebs*)
The pinky-brown male, with its grey cap and black-and-white striped wings, is another easily recognised bird. The pattern of the female's plumage is similar but in light shades of brown.

Greenfinch (*Carduelis chloris*)
Living up to its name, the male Greenfinch is green (with yellow stripes on its wings and tail). The female, regrettably, is a tawny brown.

Goldfinch (*Carduelis carduelis*)
Once seen, never forgotten, with its red face and bright golden panels on its wings, as if it were the winner in a paint-by-numbers competition.

Hawfinch (*Coccothraustes coccothraustes*)
A very colourful bird but a tricky one to observe, since it is not only rare but tends to keep to Beech woods. Look for the chestnut head, buff undersides and almost parrot-like bill.

EASY NATURE

Just remember this:
Finches derive their name from the
'fink' sound the Chaffinch makes.

A Goldfinch

For future study – the finches you may not know to be finches

All the following are bona fide members of the finch family, despite the fact that the suffix '–finch' does not occur in their name. Of them, the yellowy Siskin, the red-capped Redpoll and the pink-breasted Linnet are the most likely to come swooping across your path: **Brambling** (*Fringilla montifringilla*), **Crossbill** (*Loxia curvirostra*), **Linnet** (*Carduelis cannabina*), **Redpoll** (*Carduelis flammea*), **Serin** (*Serinus serinus*), **Siskin** (*Carduelis spinus*) and **Twite** (*Carduelis flavirostris*).

The bill for the meal

The food required by each sort of finch determines its bill shape.

Bullfinch – *rounded* bill: for dealing with soft fruits and buds.

Chaffinch – *sharp* bill: for eating insects, caterpillars and sun flower seeds.

Goldfinch – *pointed* bill: for picking out seeds from thistles and the like.

Greenfinch – *large* bill: for taking on hard fruits such as Dog Rose-hips.

Hawfinch – *immense* bill: for smashing open hard stones like cherries.

What you should say:

'No Goldfinches in your garden?
Try giving them some niger seeds –
they're like tiny Goldfinch magnets.'

Fair game?

Gamebirds have short legs, short curved bills and plump bodies. They spend an uncomfortable amount of their short lives being shot at by men (usually) with seemingly nothing better to do with their lives than render meaningless violence unto other living things. Bring on the day when such people are forced to fly slowly about ten to fifteen feet above rows of birds who blast their guts out with shotguns and have their wounded bodies picked up in the drooling mouths of Retrievers.

The pheasants

Common Pheasant
(*Phasianus colchicus*)
The male is a colourful bird with red eye-patches, dark green head, russet plumage and a long tail reminiscent of the tail on a kite. The female is similar in build, but pale brown with black markings.
Length: to 90cm.
Wingspan: to 90cm.

A Common Pheasant

Grey Partridge
(*Perdix perdix*) and **Red-legged Partridge** (*Alectoris rufa*)
Significantly smaller, the Grey Partridge also has a distinctive orangey-brown face, while the **Red-legged Partridge** possesses a red bill as well as red legs, and a white chin. *Length:* to 30cm. *Wingspan:* to 50cm.

A Quail

Quail
(*Coturnix coturnix*)
The eggs of a Quail have long been a delicacy associated with the upper classes. The bird that lays them is the runt among gamebirds, but has an attractive chocolate-ripple plumage. *Length:* to 18cm. *Wingspan:* to 35cm.

The grouse

Red Grouse (*Lagopus lagopus scoticus*)
About half the size of a Pheasant, more chicken-like in shape, and a herbivore. A uniquely British sub-species of the Willow Grouse, the male is a dark russet, with the female a lighter brown. Both have red 'eyebrows' (actually called *wattles*). *Length:* to 40cm. *Wingspan:* to 65cm.

A Red Grouse

Black Grouse (*Tetrao tetrix*)
Similar in size to the Red Grouse but chubbier. The male is black with a very showy white tail. The female looks similar to the female Red Grouse but has a whitish tail.

Capercaillie (*Tetrao urogallus*)
Now found only in north-east Scotland. Look for the male's fantastic black beard or the female's orange chest. Hunting of the bird is currently banned due to a recent catastrophic drop in numbers. *Length:* to 55cm. *Wingspan:* to 80cm.

Details of another grouse, the **Ptarmigan**, can be found on p. 186.

EASY NATURE

Just remember this:

Most gamebirds you might inadvertently startle from their hidey-holes in the undergrowth will either be Pheasants or Red Grouse. These two birds are quite different, so it's just a case of asking yourself whether the individual looks like the bird on the label of The Famous Grouse whisky bottle. If the event has occurred in southern England, you've seen a Pheasant.

• The so-called 'Glorious 12th' refers to the first day (12 August) of the open season on grouse.

What you should say:

'One grouse, two grice.'

Seven Geese for seven ganders

A wedge of migrating geese cruising overhead is one of the great sights of nature. Some might also argue that the mass honking of Canada Geese is one of the great sounds of nature too. Since Britain lays claim to but seven members of the goose family (whether resident or visitor), there is every chance of being able to memorise the entire set – it's merely a question of matching the markings to the goose.

Markings: Grey-brown plumage, a white rump, large orange bill and pinkish legs.
Species: **Greylag Goose** (*Anser anser*)
Also note: Very common. The ancestor of the domesticated goose.

A Greylag Goose

Markings: Black-and-white head, black neck, brown body and black legs.
Species: **Canada Goose** (*Branta canadensis*)
Also note: A frequent sight in public parks. Originally introduced from Canada as an ornamental bird.

Markings: Black-and-white head, black neck, white belly, black and grey wings.
Species: **Barnacle Goose** (*Branta leucopsis*)
Also note: This is the only goose without a hint of brown on it. Caerlaverock, on the Solway Firth, is the winter quarters of the entire population that lives on the Norwegian island of Svalbard.

Markings: Mainly dark brown with white at the front of the head.
Species: **White-fronted Goose** (*Anser albifrons*)
Also note: Another winter visitor from the Arctic.

Markings: Similar to a Greylag Goose but with pink legs and a pink band on the bill.
Species: **Pink-footed Goose** (*Anser brachyrhynchus*)
Also note: Yet another Arctic goose down for the 'warm' British winter.

Markings: Shades of brown with a white triangle at the top of the neck and a white rump.

Species: **Brent Goose** (*Branta bernicla*)

Also note: Winter visitors from the Arctic tundra, they are found only in coastal areas.

A Brent Goose

Markings: Also like a Greylag Goose but with a broad band of orange on the bill.

Species: **Bean Goose** (*Anser fabalis*)

Also note: There are just two British Bean Goose flocks – one in the Yare Valley, Norfolk (late November to early March), and a smaller one in the Avon Valley, between Falkirk and Cumbernauld (late September to February). The bird gets its name from its tendency in the past to graze bean fields.

EASY NATURE

Just remember this:

Domesticated geese are mainly or often entirely white. Most wild geese are predominantly brown.

- The rhyme 'Goosy Goosy Gander, where dost thou wander? / Upstairs, downstairs, in my lady's chamber' is not about geese at all, but is a veiled reference to the sort of post-watershed activities that might go on in a lady's chamber.

- The Barnacle Goose gets its name from the belief that they came from Barnacles, as seen on the undersides of ships.

- The goose that laid the golden eggs is the star of Aesop's fable about the dangers of greed.

What you should say:

'According to Livy, the squawking of geese once saved Rome from a night-time attack of Gauls.'

Gulls want to be with the gulls

G ulls are a gregarious lot who love the British coastline so much that there is hardly a stretch of it that does not resound to their harsh squeals and squawks. However, it should be noted that there is no such thing as a 'Seagull'. This a loose term popularly applied to all gulls, but since all of them spend most of the time at the coast, the 'Sea' part of the name is fairly superfluous. Distance yourself from the madding crowd by ridding it from your vocabulary, except in quotation (see below). All gulls have webbed feet and pointed wings, and most are pretty fierce predators.

Three gulls

Something has gone awry with the naming of many British gulls, so it is as well to be cautious of them.

A Herring Gull

Herring Gull

(*Larus argentatus*) Although it does eat Herrings, the Herring Gull has quite a varied diet that includes small mammals, birds, shellfish and whatever it can pick up from landfill sites. This is the gull whose 'key-owk key-owk' call is the one we associate with the seaside. People who live on the coast often find them a menace, since they have taken to nesting between chimney stacks, where their size, numbers and habit of defecating on the wing make them somewhat intimidating. It's no surprise then that these are the only gulls you are ever likely to be able to befriend, for they have little fear of humans and will eat almost anything you care to throw in their direction (though you should note that many councils prohibit this practice). They have grey wings, tipped with black, and their white heads become streaked with grey in winter. *Length:* to 65cm. *Wingspan:* to 1.6m

Common Gull (*Larus canus*)
Not actually a terribly common gull in most of Britain, though
it evidently once was, and remains so in the north of Scotland.
Most likely to be seen in winter, often on farmland rather than
directly over the coast. Similar colourings to the Herring Gull
but much smaller and with greenish rather
than pink legs.
Length: 42cm.
Wingspan: 1.25cm.

Black-headed Gull
(*Larus ridibundus*)
The Black-headed
Gull's head is
actually brown in
summer and white
with two dark smudges
on each side of the head
in winter. Another landfill site visitor,

A Black-headed Gull

the Black-headed Gull favours boggy land, reservoirs and
flooded pits when inland. *Length:* to 36cm. *Wingspan:* to 1.1m

For future study

The **Little Gull** (*Larus minutus*) whose head *is* black; the
Kittiwake (*Rissa tridactyla*) whose cry is 'Kiti-waak'; the **Greater
Black-backed Gull** (*Larus marinus*) whose back is black; and
the **Lesser Black-backed Gull** (*Larus fiscus*) whose back is 'less
black' (i.e. grey).

EASY NATURE

Just remember this:

There is no such thing as a Seagull, and the
head of the Black-headed Gull is never black.

What you should say after a couple of post-dinner brandies:

'I'm a seagull. No, that's wrong. Remember
you shot a seagull? A man happened to come
along, saw it and killed it, just to pass the time.
A plot for a short story.'[1]

---

[1] *The Seagull*, Act IV, by Anton Chekhov.

Up with the Larks

If you are walking across a field and there is a long chirruping melody playing high above, you can be fairly sure that you are in the presence of a **Skylark**. Perhaps 'presence' is too strong a word because it is quite possible that you won't even be able to see the bird, which is not large and likely to be a long way up. The Skylark's astonishing song on the wing has meant that its near-namesakes, the **Woodlark** and the elusive **Shorelark**, barely get a look in, but both are worthy of study on their own merits.

A Skylark

Skylark (*Alauda arvensis*)

Should you encounter a Skylark (18cm) at a lower altitude, you'll see a rather fetching crest on its head, and brown and white markings as if someone has tipped chocolate ripple ice cream down it, with only the soft white undersides and grey underwings escaping the deluge. You might also notice the bird's long hind claw which is useful for balancing when running through long grasses.

The fall of the Skylark

Sadly, Skylark numbers have dropped by 90 per cent over the last 30 years, due largely to changes in farming practices. Skylarks nest and feed in fields of cereals sown in spring, and rely on the winter stubble of cereal crops for food. With many farmers now sowing cereals in autumn, the winter stubble has been ploughed over and the crops are too tall by the spring for the birds to nest in them.

A Woodlark

Woodlark (*Lullula arborea*)

The song of the Woodlark is considered by many to be among the loveliest of any bird. It performs from the tops of tall trees as well as on the wing. Similar in appearance to the Skylark but smaller (15cm) and without a crest, it is generally seen only in open woodlands, glades and sandy heaths in the south of England.

Shorelark (*Eremophila alpestris*)

A rare winter guest from the Arctic who settles on isolated marshes around the coast, hence its name. The Shorelark has similar markings to the Woodlark, but with a striking yellow and black face and a broad band of black under its chin.

EASY NATURE

Just remember this:
In its song flight, the Skylark ascends vertically, hovers, and then dives back to earth.

- George Meredith's poem 'The Lark Ascending' inspired Ralph Vaughan Williams to write his orchestral piece of the same name.

- The Skylark's airborne song lasts for two to three minutes, getting longer as the summer wears on.

What you should say:

'Hail to thee, blithe spirit! / Bird thou never wert.'[1]

---

[1]Opening lines of Percy Bysshe Shelley's poem 'To a Skylark'.

Magpies and Jays, crows in all but appearance

The Magpie and the Jay are two birds that even the most hesitant of birdwatchers can get under their belt. Both are crows (p. 114), but so distinctive that a positive identification is a straightforward affair. Magpies, it must be said, have shocking reputations. It is true that they are wont to eat the eggs and offspring of other birds (but then so do many other animals such as cats and Badgers), and will occasionally pick up shiny objects and carry them to their nests (but then so do most crows). However, it is humans who have anthropomorphised this behaviour and found the Magpie guilty, according to our own lights, as if the poor birds were acting out of spite. Their close relative the Jay, by comparison, has somehow managed to avoid being burdened with such a welter of opprobrium.

A Magpie

Identification

Magpies (*Pica pica*) are large (45cm), sociable and can be seen almost anywhere in Britain. Look for their black heads, white sides, and the flush of metallic blue on their wings and tail. They have a refreshingly universalist approach to food and, although much of their diet consists of insects, they will try almost anything once. On the positive side, their scavenging means they are responsible for reducing the percentage of discarded food that would otherwise become landfill. **Jays** (*Garrulus glandarius*), though slightly smaller (35cm), are extremely eye-catching with their pinky-grey bodies, a flash of blue on their wings, a white rump and black tail. They have a similarly varied diet (including nestlings) and are widespread, with the exception of northern Scotland.

A Jay

EASY NATURE

Just remember this:

Jays are the Squirrels of the air, collecting acorns in the autumn and burying them for consumption in winter when food is hard to come by.

The Magpie Rhyme

A children's rhyme suggests what the future might hold for those seeing a certain number of Magpies at the same time. The most popular of the various versions is: 'One for sorrow / Two for joy / Three for a girl / Four for a boy / Five for silver / Six for gold / Seven for a secret never to be told.'

• An old English folk saying declares: 'A single Magpie in spring, foul weather will bring.'

• When seen alone near a window in Scotland, Magpies are the harbingers of death, while in various counties of England, such as Devon, they merely bring bad luck. The usual formula to avert such misfortune is to say: 'Hello, Mr Magpie.'

What you should say:

'There are many rhymes about Magpies, but none of them is very reliable, because they are not the ones the Magpies know.'[1]

---

[1] If challenged, you should come clean and confess that you are quoting from Terry Pratchett's *Carpe Jugulum*.

The Owl, wise harbinger of death and lunacy

T he ultimate night flyer, the owl is an instantly recognisable bird, thanks to its big, heart-shaped face and round, all-seeing eyes. Britain is fortunate to play host to five species of these seemingly enigmatic birds. Although only the male Tawny (Britain's most numerous owl species) indulges in proper 'to-wit' and 'woo-hoo' cries (the female can manage only the 'to-wit'), it is reassuring that many an owl does indeed build its nest in a hollow Oak (p. 170).

What you should know about owls

i.   Like woodpeckers (p. 158), owls have two toes on each foot pointing forwards and two pointing backwards. This is handy for gripping on to tree trunks and the like.

ii. Both their hearing and eyesight are exceptional (though they cannot see in pitch darkness).

iii. If spotted during the daytime, they are liable to be subjected to mob attacks by mixed groups of small birds clubbing together for a pre-emptive strike.

Barn Owl (*Tyto alba*)

Look for: Brilliant white underwings and belly, and vaguely striped fawn wings.

Diet: Voles, mice, rats and shrews.

Preferred nesting site: A barn or a capacious hole in an old tree.

Out and about: Often begins hunting just before dusk.

Tawny Owl (*Strix aluco*)

Look for: Mainly brown body and wings with spots of white, and paler mottled belly.

Diet: Mice, rats, voles, small birds, worms, frogs and beetles.

Preferred nesting site: Barn, tree or old Crows' nest.

Out and about: Nocturnal (sometimes feeding on rodents in city centres).

Short-eared Owl (*Asio flammeus*)

Look for: Similar markings to Tawny Owl but with face less obviously split into two halves. Flies low over open ground when hunting.

Diet: Voles, other small mammals, small birds, large insects.

Preferred nesting site: A barely defined scrape on the ground.

Out and about: The only British owl that frequently hunts in good daylight (mainly during the evening).

You should also be aware of

The other two British owls: the nocturnal **Long-eared Owl** (*Asio otus*) which is similar in appearance to the Short-eared Owl but with longer ears; and the **Little Owl** (*Athene noctua*) which is Britain's smallest owl (around 23cm in length – roughly two-thirds the size of the other owls).

A Tawny Owl

EASY NATURE

Just remember this:

The Barn Owl and the Tawny Owl have black eyes – all the others have yellow-orange ones.

• The jury is out on what owls 'mean': in many cultures they are associated with calamity and death, while others see them as the personification of wisdom. The Finns, bless them, think of the owl as representing both wisdom and idiocy.

What you should say:

'Owls … represent the stark twilight and unsatisfied thoughts which all [people] have.'[1]

[1] Henry David Thoreau, *Walden*.

Rats with wings

To many people (particularly town councillors), pigeons are a nuisance fit only for extermination or, at the very least, being moved on. Their propensity to drive out other birds, excrete on every available surface, and generally get underfoot has made them enemies from London's Trafalgar Square to Sydney's Martin Place. Lest we forget, however, not so long ago there was a tradition in many British cities of buying seed (though not always at twopence a bag) specifically to feed the pigeons, an act which is now banned or greatly discouraged. Pigeons are thus often reduced to picking at cigarette butts, a habit that has led them to be known in some quarters as 'flying ashtrays'.

'Pigeons'

A Rock Dove

It should be emphasised that there is technically no such bird as simply a 'Pigeon'. What people are nearly always refer-ring to when they use the term is a feral **Rock Dove** (*Columba livia*). These are birds that have adapted well to modern urban life, finding the tall buildings of cities a good substitute for the cliff-top abodes of their ancestors. They come in a wide range of markings, but in cities almost everything you see that looks like a pigeon will be a feral Rock Dove.

Pigeons that are not 'Pigeons'

The pigeon family encompasses a number of attractive birds, including the smarter but similar-looking **Stock Dove** (*Columba oenas*); the pink-breasted **Turtle Dove** (*Streptopelia turtur*); the pale manila **Collared Dove** (*Streptopelia decaocto*) with a thin black 'collar' at the back of its neck; the **Woodpigeon** (*Columba palumbus*), best known for its woodland cooing song; and the now much less numerous cliff-dwelling **Rock Dove** (*Columba livia*), from whom the 'pigeon' is descended.

A Turtle Dove

EASY NATURE

Just remember this:

In Britain there are an estimated 18 million feral Rock Doves (as you have now started to call them).

- Pigeons have been raced in Britain since 1881.

- In Afghanistan, the keeping of pigeons was banned under the Taliban.

- Over 100,000 homing pigeons (domesticated Rock Doves) were used during the First World War to carry messages, and anyone in Britain found to have shot one faced a possible six-month prison sentence.

- Although there have been some health-scare stories regarding feral Rock Doves, there is no evidence to suggest that they can pass on diseases to humans.

- The first-ever commercial airmail service was a Pigeon Post established in New Zealand in 1897. Tiny messages could be sent from Great Barrier Island to Auckland (but not the other way).

What you should say:
'Pigeons on the grass alas.'[1]

---

[1]Gertrude Stein, *Four Saints in 3 Acts*, Act III, Scene ii.

On the Rails

Rails are relatively long-legged birds that are a good deal happier on the water than on land, and often seem troubled by the intricacies of flight. The exception to this rule is the **Corncrake** (*Crex crex*), a rare mottled fawn bird that is more often found on farmland. The two most populous rails in Britain are the Moorhen and the Coot, both of which are frequent sights on lakes, large ponds and slow-moving rivers.

Moorhen (*Gallinula chloropus*)

Unlike the Coot, which has no qualms about swimming across open water, the Moorhen prefers to hunt and bathe in less exposed stretches, such as where a tree may have fallen. A very dark brown or slate grey except for the odd fleck of white, the Moorhen is most easily identified by its red bill (which has a yellow tip). *Length:* to 35cm.

A Coot

Coot (*Fulica atra*)

Like the Moorhen, the Coot is widespread but for the far north-west of Scotland. Although it's roughly the same length as the Moorhen, it is a much bigger bird (usually weighing two to three times as much), with a black body, a dab of white on its face, and a gleaming white bill. Thus there really are no excuses for any uncertainty. *Length:* to 37cm.

Great Crested Grebe
(*Podiceps cristatus*)

Not a rail, but a bird often seen in the same habitats as the Moorhen and Coot, the Great Crested Grebe resembles an earnest vicar peering out over an imaginary lectern. The adults have a very distinctive double crest on top of their heads with a dramatic sharp bill and a white-and-orange face. Their offspring are a wonder to behold, and well worth looking out for in spring – fluffy little things when very young, with zebra stripes from head to tail. They are wont to climb onto their mother's back and wait impatiently for their father to bring them food. *Length:* to 50cm.

A Great Crested Grebe

EASY NATURE

Just remember this:

If you're still not sure whether you're looking at a Moorhen or a Coot, remember that *henna* is red (well, reddish), as is the Moor*hen*'s bill.

- In a reversal of the normal state of affairs, female Moorhens will fight each other for the honour of mating with a particular male.
- Coots are excellent underwater swimmers and it is fun to watch them 'duck dive' and guess where they might break the surface again, popping up like a cork.

What you should say:

'i come from haunts of coot and hern / i make a sudden sally / and-er-hem-er-hem the fern / to bicker down a valley.'[1]

[1]Alfred, Lord Tennyson, 'The Brook', as doctored by Geoffrey Willans in *Down with Skool.*

The rapture of raptors (part i)

There are two major problems when it comes to identifying birds of prey (raptors): i) they tend to fly too high to see them properly; and ii) too many of them just look like eagles. Worse still, there is such a mystique about eagles that if you should ever see one and correctly identify it as such, there is very little chance that any less knowledgeable companions lucky enough to be in your presence will actually believe you. However, there is no denying the wonder and awe inspired by a bird of prey circling on invisible thermals high above, so actually being able to name it is more the icing on the cake than the cake itself.

Features that raptors have in common

Bills – all raptors have more or less the same design: a curved tip and lethally sharp edges for ripping apart their victims.

Talons – claws (usually three forwards and one back) that can be used to kill by crushing.

How to tell one raptor from the next

If it's relatively small

Merlin (*Falco columbiarus*)

Britain's smallest raptor. Low-flying.

Wingspan:
60–65cm.

A Merlin

Sparrowhawk (*Accipiter nisus*)

Round wings but a very long tail. Typically seen soaring above woodland. Yellow eyes.
Wingspan: 60–75cm.

A Kestrel

A Hobby

Kestrel (*Falco tinnunculus*)

Britain's commonest raptor. Look for it hovering over roadside verges as if on a piece of string. Black eyes.
Wingspan: 65–80cm.

Hobby (*Falco subbuteo*)

Very elegant, and sporting what look like orange shorts and a black moustache.
Wingspan: 70–85cm.

See The rapture of raptors (part ii) *overleaf.*

The rapture of raptors *(part ii)*

How to tell one raptor from the next

If it's medium-sized

Peregrine
(*Falco peregrinus*)
Yellow feet, yellow ring
around the eye, yellow
flash above the bill,
and white breast.
Wingspan: 95–115cm.

Goshawk (*Accipiter gentilis*)
Soars over forests; with
whitish undersides and
a white stripe over each eye.
Wingspan: 100–115cm.

A Peregrine

A Hen Harrier

Hen Harrier
(*Circus cyaneus*)
Low-flying and
slow. Male mostly
light grey with
black wing tips
and white breast.
Female brown
with a white rump.
Wingspan:
100–120cm.

Marsh Harrier (*Circus aeruginosus*)
Found in reed beds from the Fens to Kent, locally in south-west and north-west England, and on the coasts of south Wales.
Wingspan: 110–125cm.

Buzzard (*Buteo buteo*)

Makes a mewing sound while swirling around on thermals.
Wingspan: 115–125cm.

If it's large

Honey Buzzard (*Pernis apivorus*)

Chocolate brown with brown-and-white striped undersides
(but not a true Buzzard).
Wingspan: 135–150cm.

Osprey (*Pandion haliaetus*)

Eats fish, so often seen by water. Noticeable white head
with a black stripe from each eye to the neck.
Wingspan: 145–160cm.

Red Kite (*Milvus milvus*)

A very obvious forked tail (the
upper side of which is red).
Wingspan: 145–165cm.

A Red Kite

If it's huge

It is a **Golden Eagle**
(*Aquila chrysaetos*)
Wingspan: 190–225cm.

Owls (p. 130) are also raptors, but so distinctive that there is
rarely a problem with identification.

EASY NATURE

Just remember this:

Raptors have three eyelids – a top, a bottom and
a transparent one that goes from side to side.

• The Subbuteo football game, being a sort of 'hobby', was named
  after the Hobby (*Falco subbuteo*).

What you should say:

'Female raptors are generally larger than males, but no one's quite sure why.'

Large sea birds that are not gulls

B y no means all large sea birds are gulls. Gannets, Shearwaters, Cormorants and Auks all cast long shadows on our beaches and cliff-tops and fill the skies with their rasping chorus. Memorising just half a dozen of them is a good start to any trip to the coast.

If you see a particularly large sea bird it might be

The **Northern Gannet** (*Morus bassanus*), usually just known as the Gannet, is the largest seabird in Europe. That, combined with its yellowish head, white body and white black-tipped wings, and its propensity to dive at tremendous speed into the sea in search of fish, means that there's nothing in the sky that can be confused with it. Actually seeing one is the tricky part, because their colonies are often found on tiny and remote offshore islands, particularly off Scotland. *Length:* to 90cm. *Wingspan:* to 1.8m.

The **Cormorant** (*Phalacrocorax carbo*) – identifiable by its jet-black body and wings, white chin and yellow patch at the base of its bill, the Cormorant is another giant of the shoreline. Can be seen almost anywhere along the coast, but also frequents inland bodies of water across England and Wales. *Length:* to 1m. *Wingspan:* to 1.6m.

The **Shag** (*Phalacrocorax aristotelis*) – similar-looking (though with a crest on the top of its head and no white chin) but smaller than the Cormorant, the Shag is another incessant diver into the waters off Scotland and Wales, and NE and SW England. *Length:* to 80cm. *Wingspan:* to 1.05m.

A more modest sea bird might be

The **Guillemot** (*Uria aalge*), which spends much of its lifetime at sea, touching land only to breed. It's basically black on top and white underneath. *Length:* to 55cm. *Wingspan:* to 70cm.

The **Fulmar** (*Fulmarus glacialis*), an astonishingly successful bird. Unknown in Britain before 1878, there are now estimated to be over a million along the coast. Superficially similar to the Herring Gull (p. 124), but with a noticeably stubby hooked bill. *Length:* to 50cm. *Wingspan:* to 1.1m.

However, there is only one

Atlantic Puffin (*Fratercula arctica*), with its huge beak and sad, clown-like eyes. *Length:* to 30cm. *Wingspan:* to 60cm.

An Atlantic Puffin

EASY NATURE

Just remember this:

The average Puffin can fit ten fish in its bill at once.

• The **Great Auk** (*Pinguinus impennis*), which was flightless and unafraid of people, was driven to global extinction by its human friends. The last Great Auk in Britain was killed on Stac an Armin, St Kilda, in 1840, by two locals who reportedly believed it was a witch.

What you should say:

'The Northern Gannet is a protected species, but the inhabitants of Port Nis on the Isle of Lewis are permitted to sail annually to the island of Sula Sgeir to kill up to 2,000 of the birds to eat.'

The ones that get away

Thence are some birds, such as the doughty Robin (p. 150), that everyone seems to be able to recognise more or less from birth, yet others, such as the House Sparrow or the Wren, which are common but somehow manage to flummox people. There can be few things more humiliating for the *soi disant* naturalist than to be caught out by a commonplace creature, so look upon a little study (or revision) as protection against such disasters.

A Wren

Nailing the 'simple' birds

Wren (*Troglodytes troglodytes*)

Tiny birds (no longer than 10cm) that sing like there's no tomorrow.

Identified by: Very stubby tail cocked at an angle, with bursts of amazingly fast bee-like wing beats when flying.

European Starling (*Sturnus vulgaris*)

A bird that, no matter whether seen in its summer or winter coat, always looks like it has recently bathed in an oil slick.

Identified by: Light brown spots, like chicken pox, on a dark brown or black body. Famed for flocking in huge numbers in winter.

Sparrows

Once among the commonest of British garden birds, Sparrows are now routinely outnumbered in the hedgerows of suburbia by Blackbirds (p. 150), Chaffinches (p. 118) and Tits (p. 152). However, there are still enough of them around to make it essential that you can put a name to them with something approaching confidence.

House Sparrow (*Passer domesticus*)

Identified by: A grey crown, white cheeks, and black throat in the case of the male; females have a slightly trickier fawn underside, mottled brown uppers and a pale stripe behind the eye as sometimes sported by (human) female Goths.

Tree Sparrow (*Passer montanus*)

Identified by: Its House Sparrow looks coupled with a brown cap (looking embarrassingly like a mullet) and a black splodge on each white cheek.

A Starling

The ones that get away *cont.*

Wagtails

Conveniently, a family of birds that give their long pencil-thin tails a pronounced wag. If you suspect that you have seen a Wagtail, it's just a matter of sorting out which one it is. Less conveniently, the names of three of them are poor indicators of how to do this.

A Pied Wagtail

Pied Wagtail (*Motacilla alba yarrellii*) – British sub-species of the White Wagtail

Identified by: Stark black and white markings, as the name suggests.

A Grey Wagtail

White Wagtail (*Motacilla alba alba*)
Identified by: Grey back (with black and white markings elsewhere).

Grey Wagtail (*Motacilla cinerea*)
Identified by: Grey back, like the White Wagtail, but also yellow underparts including a magnificent yellow rump.

Yellow Wagtail (*Motacilla flava*)
Identified by: A yellow belly, like the Grey Wagtail, but also an olive green head (happily, there is no Green Wagtail to muddy the waters further).

A Yellow Wagtail

EASY NATURE

Just remember this:

The Wren's Latin name means 'cave dweller', after its habit of hunting for food in nooks and crannies (and caves, if it can find any).

What you should say:

'Teach your parrot whatever words
you will, "I'll have a starling shall be taught to
speak / Nothing but 'Mortimer'."'[1]

---

[1] *Henry IV Part I*, Act I, Scene iii.

The large wetland birds

Beautiful though many of the smaller birds are, there's nothing to match the sheer elegance of a Swan or Heron passing overhead on wings that go on for ever.[1] Wherever there is a stretch of water, look out for a Mute Swan or a Grey Heron getting on with its relatively untroubled and, for the most part, unhurried life.

Mute Swan

The familiar long neck of the **Mute Swan** (*Cygnus olor*) is used for reaching down into the shallows to feed on vegetation, and you'll often see them up-ending themselves in the water with only their tails showing in order to poke their orange bills down further. Their all-white plumage makes them visible for great distances and warns other swans to stay off their territory. *Wingspan:* 210–240cm.

Other swans

The **Whooper Swan** (*Cygnus cygnus*) is generally seen north of the English Midlands, and though the same size and shape as the Mute Swan, can be easily distinguished by its black-tipped yellow bill. The **Bewick's Swan** (*Cygnus bewickii*), however, is noticeably smaller and looks more like a very large white Goose.

Grey Heron

Never has grey been so decorously worn as on the wings of the **Grey Heron** (*Ardea cinerea*). Often seen standing motionless in the shallows of a stream waiting for an unwary fish, frog or rodent to pass by, the Grey Heron's call sounds like it's permanently asking after someone called 'Frank'. *Wingspan:* 175–195cm.

Other herons

The **Little Egret** (*Egretta garzetta*) has a Grey Heron's legs and bill (though in black) coupled with the shape and sheer whiteness of a Mute Swan. With a wingspan of 90–105cm, it does not look out of place among the Grey Heron with which it sometimes mingles in southern England. The **Bittern** (*Botaurus stellarus*), meanwhile, resembles a plump Grey Heron painted a buff brown with black streaks and with slightly shorter wings. Its range is strictly restricted to wet reed

[1]Not literally.

A Little Egret

beds. The **Little Bittern** (*Ixobrychus minutus*) is a very much smaller bird, black on top with pale undersides, and very occasionally visits southern England in spring.

EASY NATURE

Just remember this:

Mute Swans are so called because they are, as a rule, silent (although they will hiss if feeling threatened).

- All wild swans in Britain have been protected by Royal Charter and have belonged to the reigning monarch since the 12th century.

- In some parts of England, Grey Herons are known as 'Cranes' (though they are *not* Cranes (*Grus grus*)).

- Swans usually mate for life, though there are occasional recorded instances of swan couples splitting up.

What you should say:

'Yes, thank you, I was aware that a swan can break a man's arm with its wing.'

The swoopingness of Swallows, Swifts and Martins

I f a bird goes swooping around you in summer like a paper aeroplane, the chances are it is a Swallow, a Swift or a Martin. Despite the similarities between the first two (Martins are much smaller, so easy to identify), you should not make the schoolboy/girl error of thinking that they are from the same family. Swallows (and Martins) are Hirundinidae, while Swifts are Apodidae. All three spend their winters in sub-Saharan Africa, and make the long and dangerous journey each year to summer in Europe, with pairs very often nesting in exactly the same place as in previous years.

Swallow
(*Hirundo rustica*)

A Swallow

Heaven help the Swallow if Britain's telephone service ever goes completely wireless, because roughly 5 million of them spend huge amounts of time congregating on the wires stretched between telegraph poles. Look for their distinctive red chins when lined up on these perches. They build mud nests under the eaves of buildings or anywhere else that will give adequate protection from predators and the weather.

Swift (*Apus apus*)

The advent of Swifts (and Swallows) in Britain traditionally heralds the beginning of summer. However, rather than making their usual appearance in mid-May, in 2007 the first Swifts began arriving in mid-April – apparently a consequence of global warming. Swifts have tiny feet on which all four tiny toes point forward, thus making it impossible for them to perch on wires.

House Martin (*Delichon urbica*)

Beautiful creatures with bluey-black backs and, in flight, much more shallowly forked tails than the Swallow or Swift. As their name suggests, they nest under the eaves of houses.

Sand Martin (*Riparia riparia*)

Small sandy brown birds whose name is derived from their habit of setting up colonies in sand banks (although they will often make do with banks of earth, railway cuttings or the sides of gravel pits).

Telling a Swift from a Swallow from a Martin			
	Undersides	*Telephone wires*	*Approximate length*
Swallow	White	Yes	18cm
Swift	Dark brown	No	17cm
Martin	White	Yes	12cm

EASY NATURE

Just remember this:

A simple way to tell a Swift from a Swallow in flight is that the Swallow has milky-white underparts (and milk is something nice to *swallow*).

- The technical term for the practice of passing a summer in a particular place is 'to aestivate'. This will sound good when using it of birds, but a tad pretentious in the sentence: 'Gerald and I hope to aestivate in a caravan at Torquay this year.'

- Swallows, Swifts and Martins arrive in Britain in dribs and drabs but leave in early autumn in large flocks. Like other migrating birds, they do most of their migrating at night.

What you should say:

'One Swallow may not traditionally be thought to make a summer, but it certainly makes mine.'

The celebrity-strewn thrush family

As with many other bird families (herons and crows, for instance), Thrushes are not the only thrushes. Indeed, they are arguably not even the most famous or illustrious birds in the family that bears their name, being upstaged by Robins, Blackbirds and Nightingales. Many thrushes are very common visitors to gardens, which explains why they have become some of the best-known British birds.

Four common thrushes

Song Thrush (*Turdus philomelos*)

A stocky bird (to 23cm), the Song Thrush (often just called a Thrush) is recognisable by its beautiful light brown undersides covered with upside-down 'V'-shaped dark brown splodges that look like a tiny bird's footprints.

Mistle Thrush (*Turdus viscivorus*)

A larger (to 27cm) and more graceful version of the Song Thrush, the Mistle Thrush has very similar markings but its splodges are, on closer inspection, much rounder. As you might expect, the Mistle Thrush enjoys eating the fruit of Mistletoe and, in so doing, helps spread its seeds from tree to tree.

Blackbird (*Turdus merula*)

Undoubtedly the most important thing to remember about the Blackbird is that the female of the species is brown. The second most important thing is that young Blackbirds of either sex are also brown. Thus, only the adult male is actually *black*. A voracious insect- and Earthworm-eater, when the Blackbird (or its family) is itself in danger of becoming prey, it rattles out an astonishing and unhinged rapid-fire alarm call.

European Robin (*Erithacus rubecula*)

The cheery and very tame herald of Christmas can be seen more or less anywhere all year round, and its 'red breast' is probably the most famous part of any bird in the British Isles. There is no kudos attached to being able to identify a Robin so, if you see one, remark instead that if they manage to get through the first year of life, they've every chance of surviving to a ripe old age (anything up to ten years).

A Blackbird

A face made for radio

The **Nightingale** (*Luscinia megarhynchos*) may not merit a second look (it's a drab brown bird), but it is rightly famed for its melodious song and is immortalised in John Keats' 'Ode to a Nightingale' (albeit that the poem is really about the poet's journey into 'negative capability').

- The Mistle Thrush was once known as the 'Stormcock' on account of its habit of singing loudly during foul weather.

EASY NATURE

Just remember this:

Do not be taken in by the commonly-held belief (based no doubt on their all-black appearance) that Blackbirds are members of the crow family (p. 114).

What you should say (in the right company):

'I may be right, I may be wrong / But I'm perfectly willing to swear / That when you turned and smiled at me / A Nightingale sang in Berkeley Square.'[1]

---

[1]Eric Maschwitz and Manning Sherwin, 'A Nightingale Sang in Berkeley Square'.

The rise of the Tits

Blue Tits and Great Tits are two of the great modern success stories among British birds. Although never endangered, not so long ago the sighting of one or other was a pleasant surprise rather than an everyday occurrence. However, by adapting from a life in the woods to a life among humans – and their often generously-filled bird tables – they have transformed themselves into the commonest garden birds in many parts of the country. There are now an estimated 1.7 million breeding pairs of Great Tits in the UK, and twice that number of Blue Tits. Their less garden-centric cousins are not as abundant but boast very steady populations all the same.

A Blue Tit

The tits you are likely to see in the garden

Blue Tit (*Parus caeruleus*)
Very appealing and often scruffy-looking little balls of colour, whose sky-blue crowns lend them their name. A great eater of aphids, much to the delight of gardeners, if not aphids.

Great Tit (*Parus major*)
'Great' on account of it being one of the larger tits, and easily distinguishable from the Blue Tit because of its size and the fact that the upper part of its head is black.

The tit you may see if you are lucky

Coal Tit (*Parus ater*)
Decked out in monochrome colours, as its name suggests, but with a splash of yellow on each side of the body. The Coal Tit loves conifer trees (p. 166) but will frequent gardens at a push.

The tits you will have to go out of your way to see

Crested Tit (*Parus cristatus*), **Long-tailed Tit** (*Aegithalos caudatus*), **Marsh Tit** (*Parus palustris*) and **Willow Tit** (*Parus montanus*).

A simple guide to tit recognition

Tit	Distinguishing feature/s
Blue	Blue head
Coal	Tiny; coal-grey wings with two white bars
Crested	Crest on head
Great	Greater size; blue wings
Long-tailed	Prodigiously long tail
Marsh	Two-tone head; light brown body
Willow	As Marsh Tit but song is a merry warble

EASY NATURE

Just remember this:

If you are looking at some tits from below and cannot be sure whether they are Blue Tits or Great Tits, look at their breasts – the Great Tit has a thick black line down the centre.

- Great Tits will swarm around peanut feeders, while Blue Tits are partial to sunflower seeds.

- Blue Tits were hailed by the media of the 1960s as advanced thinkers when it was discovered that they were teaching each other the trick of pecking open milk bottles left on doorsteps in order to drink the cream floating on the top.

- Tits are tiny birds – most are no longer than 12cm, and a full-size Great Tit measures only 14cm.

What you should say on spying a Willow Tit:

'On a tree by a river a little tom-tit / Sang "Willow, tit willow, tit willow."'[1]

---

[1] From *The Mikado* by Gilbert and Sullivan.

Wading in

Wading birds, because they have to do a lot of wandering (and poking) around in water, are popularly characterised as having long thin legs and long thin bills. While there are many species like this, others – such as the Ringed Plover and the Lapwing – buck the trend and get along very well with shorter extremities. Many waders are summer visitors, preferring the warmth of Africa in the winter, but the commoner species such as the Curlew, Lapwing, Oystercatcher and Ringed Plover are made of sterner stuff and so can be seen all year round.

Five waders you should get to know

Small

Common Sandpiper (*Actitis hypoleucos*)

Mottled brown above with white undersides.

Look out for: A long tail but a short brown bill.

Length: To 20cm.

Typical habitat: Beside lakes, rivers and streams.

Location: Widespread, but rare in central and south-east England.

A Common Sandpiper

Ringed Plover (*Charadrius hiaticula*)

As its name suggests, it has rings of black and white around its head and upper body. Lower down, it is sandy coloured, with a white belly and orange legs.

Look out for: Its short orange and black bill. (Not to be confused with the **Little Ringed Plover** (*Charadrius dubius*), which is smaller (to about 15cm) and has less colourful legs.)

Length: To 20cm.

Typical habitat: Sandy shorelines.

Location: Most coastal regions.

A Lapwing

Medium

Lapwing (*Vanellus vanellus*)

An arresting bird with a black body and face, white head and undersides, and a short black bill.

Look out for: An extraordinary black crest shooting backwards off the top of its head.

Length: To 30cm.

Typical habitat: Moorland, marshes, estuaries and arable farmland.

Location: Widespread except in the Highlands of Scotland.

Wading in cont.

Oystercatcher (*Haematopus ostralegus*)

A very gregarious bird that gathers in enormous flocks whose squawking can drown out passing aeroplanes. It has a stocky black body, white undersides and pink legs.

Look out for: Its straight, bright orange bill, which looks like someone has thrust a miniature traffic cone onto the front of its face.

Length: To 45cm.

Typical habitat: Sandy or rocky beaches, occasionally on damp meadows.

Location: Mostly coastal, sometimes inland in the north.

An Oystercatcher

Large

Curlew (*Numenius arquata*)

One of the songs in the Curlew's repertoire is its own name – listen for a drawn-out cuuuur-lew.

Look out for: Streaked brown back, mottled lighter brown belly and long bill curving gently downwards.

Length: To 60cm

Typical habitat: Breeds on riverside meadows, damp moors, bogs; winters on the coast, particularly in estuaries.

Location: Frequent around the coast; fairly common inland in spring/summer except in central and south-east England.

For future study:

Other waders include the **Avocet** (*Recurvirostra avosetta*), **Dunlin** (*Calidris alpini*), **Golden Plover** (*Pluvialis apricaria*), **Redshank** (*Tringa totanus*), **Whimbrel** (*Numenius phaeopus*) and **Woodcock** (*Scolopax rusticola*).

A Curlew

EASY NATURE

Just remember this:

In flight, many waders have a pale 'V' across their wings.

What you should say:

'I'll knock down the man who claims there's a better-named bird in all the country than the Whimbrel.'

Woodpeckers

Woodpeckers are very often heard before they are seen; but when they are seen, they can be nothing but woodpeckers. There are only three species in Britain and they are easy to tell apart, both by size and markings.

Green Woodpecker (*Picus viridis*)
The largest of the three British woodpeckers, the Green Woodpecker is an ant-eater. Thus, contrary to what you might expect, you are far more likely to spot one feeding on some grassy stretch than in woodland. However, it does conform to type in its choice of nest – a large hole in a tree. In late summer, the Green Woodpecker's coat turns brownish, thus affording it some camouflage among the autumn leaves. The rest of the time, the Green Woodpecker has an apple-green body, with whitish cheeks and undersides, a bright red cap on its head and a dark moustache.
Length: To 32cm.
Where: All of Britain except the northern half of Scotland.

Great Spotted Woodpecker (*Dendrocopos major*)
Middle of the three, size-wise, the Great Spotted Woodpecker has seen a rise in numbers recently which is believed to be due in part to the declining fortunes of the Starling (p. 142), with which it has a natural rivalry for nesting places. It searches out insects and larvae lurking underneath the bark of trees. Its home is made by pecking a hole (about 6cm in diameter) in a tree (the hole is not much smaller than that made by the much larger Green Woodpecker). Visually unmistakable, with a red patch on its rump and on top of its head, a light fawn belly, and black-and-white wings and face.
Length: To 23cm.
Where: All of Britain except the most northerly parts of Scotland.

Lesser Spotted Woodpecker (*Dendrocopos minor*)
Smallest of the three by some way, and further distinguishable from the Great Spotted Woodpecker by its white belly, lack of a red rump, and much larger cap of red on its head. It pecks a much more modest hole for its nest (3cm).
Length: To 15cm.
Where: Wales and the lower half of England.

EASY NATURE

Just remember this:

Many people make the mistake of referring to the Greater
Spotted Woodpecker. You, of course, will omit the –er.

A Green Woodpecker

- In spring, listen out for the 'drum rolls' of the Spotted
Woodpeckers. They can be heard for some distance because the
birds choose branches which best amplify their bills' percussive
efforts.

- You can tell the male Green Woodpecker from the female by the
red smear that the former has across his moustache.

What you should say:

'In Shropshire, they believe that a
woodpecker singing loudly foretells
the coming of a rain storm.'

Trees with catkins

C atkins may seem too cylindrical and fluffy to be flowers but that is just what they are, and many of Britain's commonest trees bear them, so it's best to get used to the idea as soon as possible. Also known as *aments*, they may differ wildly in shape and size but are all composed of petal-less clusters of flowers that are wind-pollinated (some trees, such as Sallow, bear either male or female catkins and rely on there being a tree of the opposite sex in the vicinity for fertilisation to take place). Given a little practice, it should be possible to tell one catkin-bearing tree from another simply by careful examination of its catkins. Other catkin-bearers include Oaks (p. 170) and Sweet Chestnuts (p. 162).

Know your catkins

Common Alder
(*Alnus glutinosa*)
Males: Yellow (turning to deep red) and drooping (to 10cm).
Females: Small red cones that turn green (to about 2cm).

Common Beech
(*Fagus sylvatica*)
Males: Yellow and round, in drooping clusters, on long stalks.
Females: Green and upright, in pairs, on short stalks.

Hazel (*Corylus avellana*)
Males: Known as lambs' tails – yellow, drooping (to 8cm), usually in pairs or triplets.

Common Alder

Females: Red and very small, producing hazelnuts in bunches.

Sallow, Pussy Willow or **Goat Willow** (*Salix caprea*)
Males: Grey turning to yellow, rugby-ball-shaped (to 2.5cm).
Females: Green and longer (to 7cm), turning white and scattering seeds in May.

Silver Birch (*Betula pendula*)
Males: Brown in winter, in groups of two or four, becoming yellow in spring (to 5cm).
Females: Green and upright in spring before turning brown and drooping. Shorter and more bulbous than the males.

Hazel

EASY NATURE

Just remember this:
The word 'catkin' comes from the obsolete 16th-century Dutch word *katteken*, meaning 'kitten'.

- The Black Poplar's long red male catkins are considered unlucky and have the nickname Devil's fingers.

What you should say:
'At 36m in height, the Meikleour Beech Hedge in Perthshire is the tallest hedge in the world. Imagine the catkins on that.'

A Tale of Two Chestnuts

I f you do not know your Horse Chestnut from your Sweet Chestnut, blame your ancestors. When the *Aesculus hippocastanum* was introduced to Britain from Turkey (probably) in the latter half of the 16th century, the Elizabethans thought that its nut (the conker) resembled that of the Sweet Chestnut (*Castanea sativa*) and, because they found they could give conkers to horses to cure their coughs, they named the tree Horse Chestnut. This was rather unfortunate, because the Sweet Chestnut is not only a different species, but is from a completely separate genus. Even a cursory glance is enough to see that the conker – a rich brown ball with a creamy topping that looks good enough to eat but is inedible (unless you're a deer, cow, sheep or horse) – is very different from the chestnut, which is flatter and pointed and which we can eat. Furthermore, the Horse Chestnut produces tall candelabras of white (or reddy-pink) flowers, while the Sweet Chestnut is garlanded with yellowy catkins, so there's really no excuse for getting the two mixed up.

EASY NATURE

Just remember this:
Horse chestnuts produce conkers
with which to *horse* around.

A conker

The Horse Chestnut

*A couple of ways of hardening
a conker:*

- Soak it in vinegar
- Bake it in the oven

The many-fingered Horse Chestnut

MORE EASY NATURE

The Sweet Chestnut

Remember this too:

A test for differentiating between a conker and a chestnut: If you *don't* prick your fingers on the outer green casing, you're opening a conker.

The Sweet Chestnut's single saw toothed finger

How to make chestnut purée

- Gather (October/November), shell and peel your chestnuts.
- Boil in a light stock for 40 minutes.
- Mash them up.

When seen:	All year. Both lose their leaves in autumn.
Where seen:	*Horse Chestnut* – widespread, often in parks.
	Sweet Chestnut – more sporadic, with some ancient avenues planted for their nuts.

- The World Conker Championships take place in the village of Ashton, Northamptonshire, on the second Sunday of October. To avoid controversy, entrants cannot use their own conkers.

- The Sweet Chestnut is also known as the Spanish Chestnut, although it was introduced to Britain by the Romans.

- Before the Horse Chestnut came to Britain, 'conkers' (or 'conquerors') was played with hazelnuts or even snail shells. The word 'conker' may actually come from a dialect word for a 'conch' shell.

- Chestnut Sunday occurs each year on the Sunday nearest to 11 May.

What you should say:

'I came. I saw. I conkered.'

Easy trees

Even those who claim not to be able to put a name to a single tree by sight, when confronted with a branch of **Holly**, will exclaim, 'Well, of course, that's Holly. I didn't mean I couldn't name *easy* trees.' If you are just setting out on the naturalist trail, it does the heart a lot of good to realise that you actually know far more than you think you know. For this reason, there are included here four easily recognisable trees. Of course, although being able to identify trees is a good start, it's always a happier state of affairs if you know something about the trees beyond their names, so memorising one simple fact for each one should start you on your way.

Sycamore (*Acer pseudoplatanus*)

What makes them easy: Those 'helicopters' that whirl through the air in autumn, producing countless seedlings in spring.
Sycamore fact: It's a Maple tree that stands up well to pollution, which is why it is so often seen in cities.

Weeping Willow
(*Salix x chrysocoma*)

What makes them easy: They bend over, trailing their branches into rivers, streams and lakes.
Weeping Willow fact: It's a hybrid between a White Willow (*Salix alba*) and a Peking Willow (*Salix babylonica*), the latter being a popular tree in Chinese burial grounds.

Sycamore

Holly (*Ilex aquifolium*)

What makes them easy: Their Christmassy leaves and berries.
Holly fact: The wood of the Holly tree has traditionally been used to make the white pieces of a chess set (with ebony for the black pieces).

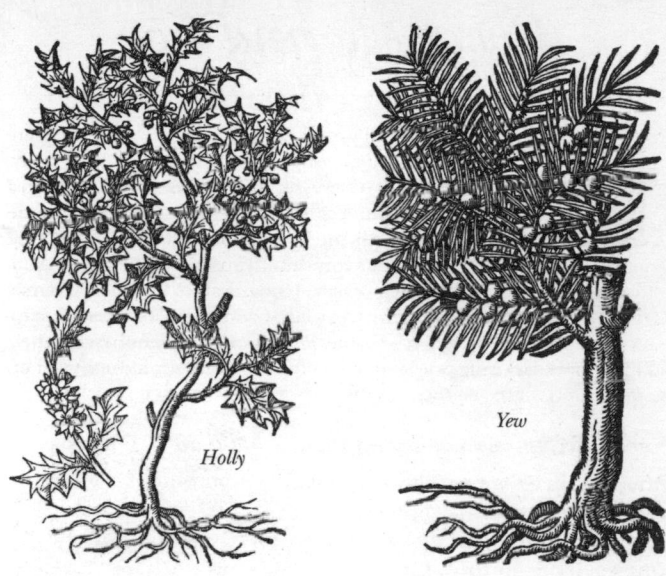

Holly

Yew

Yew (*Taxus baccata*)

What makes them easy: Practically every churchyard in Britain seems to have one.

Yew fact: Some of the planet's oldest living things are Yews. The Ashbrittle Yew in Somerset could be up to 4,000 years old; while the Fortingall Yew in Perthshire has been variously quoted as being between 2,000 and 5,000 years old.

What you should say:

'There are so many Yews in churchyards because the tree was worshipped by pagans, and churches were often built on top of sacred pagan sites. Also, it is believed that Yews were planted in churchyards to placate pagans whose religion had been suppressed. Furthermore, its leaves are poisonous to cattle, so they had to be planted somewhere the animals couldn't get to them. Look, are you listening?'

Evergreen and not quite so evergreen

The image that invariably springs to mind when one thinks of a wood is that of a grove of deciduous trees, bursting into life in the spring and painting the floor golden brown in autumn. However, this overlooks the fact that Britain is home to a broad spectrum of evergreens, from Cypresses to Firs, Pines to Redwoods, and Spruces to Cedars, not forgetting the churchyard Yews (p. 165). Although many of these are imports from continental Europe, there are some native species among them, so it is incorrect to see them as some lamentable foreign invasion.

Leyland Cypress (*x Cupressocyparis leylandii*)

A tree rather depressingly employed by householders who'd rather not see their neighbours. A hybrid of true and false Cypresses, the Leylandii famously inspired a section of The Anti-social Behaviour Act 2003.
Identification: Look for small (2cm), round cones and tiny yellow flowers on the tips of twigs.

Douglas Fir (*Pseudotsuga menziesii*)

Some of Britain's tallest trees are Douglas Firs – they can grow to over 50m.
Identification: A superb citrus smell and distinctive hanging shaggy cones (to 8cm).

The Christmas Tree problem

The **Norway Spruce** (*Picea abies*) is the most popular Christmas Tree in Britain, rivalled only by the non-needle-dropping **Nordmann Fir** (*Abies nordmanniana*). However, from an ecological perspective, Christmas Trees are a bit of a disaster, since the farms do nothing for bio-diversity, the trees are sprayed with an awful lot of pesticides (aside from those grown on the few organic farms), and are often transported long distances, only to be thrown out after Christmas. On the other hand, artificial trees arguably have an even more detrimental effect on the environment on account of their PVC content and because the vast majority come from the Far East. Try wrapping some tinsel around a pot plant and dedicating a tree via the Woodland Trust instead.

Scots Pine
(*Pinus sylvestris*)

Britain's only native pine. Despite its name, it can also be found on open heathland in England and Wales, and is widespread in forestry plantations.

Identification: The familiar pine cones, as thrown by schoolboys at each other for innumerable generations.

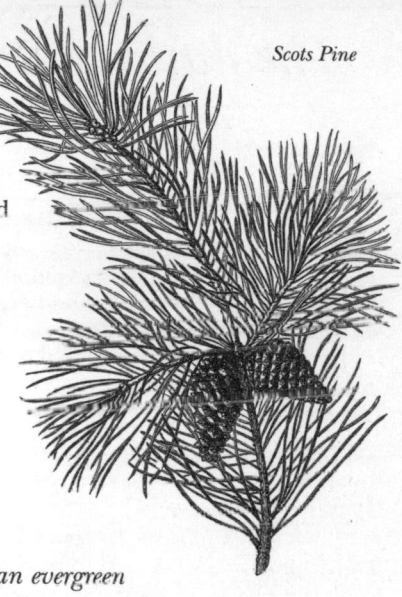

Scots Pine

Not an evergreen
European Larch (*Larix decidua*)

In summer, it looks as if it *should* be an evergreen, with its needles and cones. However, as its scientific name suggests, it is deciduous, being one of the most widespread 'winter-bare' conifers.

Identification: Branches are covered with roughly spherical sprigs of soft green needles. Rugby-ball cones (to 4cm).

European Larch

EASY NATURE

Just remember this:

The Scots Pine cones we know and love are all female ones. The male cones are thin, cylindrical and yellow.

What you should say:

'Imagine Scotland without the evergreens. Doesn't bear thinking about, does it?'

The darling buds of May

Its dense, impenetrable and thorny branches have made Hawthorn the tree of choice for hedges since the 18th century. This was when the Enclosure Acts reached their peak and huge tracts of common land fell into private hands (see p. 204). The new landowners, keen to keep the commoners out, found that Hawthorn (and occasionally Blackthorn) made a very effective barrier indeed. In the Midlands and the north of England – where almost half the land was parcelled up in this manner – the Hawthorn has become ubiquitous, so once you know what it is you will see it everywhere.

Hawthorn (*Crataegus monogyna*)

Not only does this deciduous plant make for an excellent (if somewhat bland) hedge, when allowed to grow into a tree, it is prone to be moulded by the wind into stream-lined shapes that look as if a topiarist has been at work. This is particularly true of those trees exposed to persistent strong winds as come in off the sea, for example.

Identification: Even when not used as a hedging plant, the Hawthorn rarely grows above 10m, and is usually much smaller. In winter, it can often be identified by its mass of thorny branches alone; in spring, by its distinctive leaves, cut into three or five lobes, and clusters of white flowers; and in late summer, by its volleys of bright red oval fruits.

Blackthorn (*Prunus spinosa*)

Widespread, though not as common as the Hawthorn, the Blackthorn is superficially similar in appearance but much more shrub-like and with narrow oval leaves. In summer, the Blackthorn produces *sloes* – large, spherical blue-black fruits that can be used to flavour gin.

EASY NATURE

Just remember this:
The fruit of the Hawthorn tree is called a haw.

* Hawthorn also goes by the names Whitethorn, Quickthorn, Haegthorn, and May Tree, on account of it blossoming each May. However, due to global warming, it now often flowers in April.

Hawthorn

- The Hawthorn is also called the 'bread-and-cheese' tree because poor farm labourers used to pick off the young buds to augment their meagre diet.

- Hawthorn blossom can be made into a tea which is said to be good for the heart and circulation.

- Shakespeare's 18th Sonnet makes a reference to Hawthorns: 'Rough winds do shake the darling buds of May'.

- Many species of moth depend on the Hawthorn for food.

What you should say:

'Ne'er cast a clout till may is out.'[1]

---

[1]A country saying meaning 'don't throw off your winter (or old) clothing until the Hawthorn blossoms'.

The mighty Oak

The oak, with its array of peek-a-boo roots that people think so dashing (until they stumble over them), is one of the glories of the English countryside. However, too many people imagine that there is but one oak tree, while Britain is actually home to a dozen reasonably common species.

Three common oaks

English Oak (*Quercus robur*)

One of the great symbols of England, and the inspiration behind 'Heart of Oak', the official marching song of the Royal Navy (with lyrics, somewhat surprisingly, by the 18th-century actor David Garrick). Found in great numbers in the Midlands, the English Oak can grow up to 45m high (but is usually no taller than 20m), and is renowned for often having a hollow trunk.

Leaves: On short stalks and with large lobes – the bottom two of which (called auricles) point back towards the stalk.

Male catkins: Arrive in May in short, drooping yellowy-green clusters.

Female catkins: Even shorter clusters producing minute flowers.

Acorns: Elongated (to 4cm) and brown, on long stalks.

Sessile (or Durmast) Oak (*Quercus petraea*)

Usually taller and straighter than the English Oak, the Sessile Oak often replaces it in wet upland regions, and was once used extensively for ship-building and making wine barrels.

Leaves: Similar to the English Oak, but without auricles and with significantly longer stalks.

Male catkins: Yellowy-green and drooping.

Female catkins: Hardly there at all.

Acorns: Stalkless (sessile) and green (to 3cm).

Holm Oak (*Quercus ilex*)

An evergreen oak found particularly in southern England and in coastal areas where it is used as a barrier against the worst excesses of sea winds.

Leaves: Not at all 'oaky' – long, thin, leathery and glossy.

Male catkins: Yellow and drooping, forming on young shoots.

Female catkins: Very difficult to make out.

Acorns: Small (to 2cm), green, with a pointy cream tuft.

EASY NATURE

Just remember this:

To tell the difference between an English and a Durmast Oak, remember that the former has acorns on stalks, while the latter has leaves on stalks.

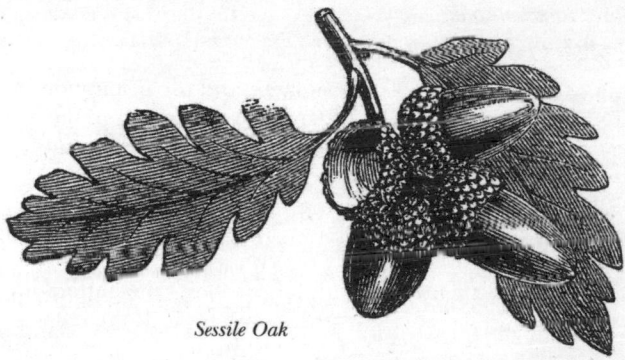

Sessile Oak

A popular rhyme gone wrong

The traditional saying, 'Oak before Ash / We're in for a splash, / Ash before Oak / We're in for a soak', suggests that if Oak flowers before the Ash, it will be a dry summer and vice versa. Sadly, tests have shown that there is no correlation between the relative flowering of the two trees and the wetness of the summer to follow.

• 'Ersatz coffee', which was drunk in the West during both world wars when coffee bean supplies were disrupted, was typically made from dried acorns.

What you should say:

'Heart of Oak are our ships, / Jolly tars are our men, / We always are ready, / Steady, boys, steady!'

Urban exotics

Towns and cities are not the first place one thinks of when seeking out the more out-of-the-ordinary species of trees. However, Britain has a noble history of carrying off spoils from foreign parts for display in its more populated spots, and from time to time these have included unusual varieties of trees, some of which have taken to urban living with surprising gusto. You might therefore keep an eye out for the following examples of exotica while wandering down even the most unpromising cul-de-sac.

Japanese Cherry (*Prunus serrulata*)

An ornamental cherry also known as an Oriental Cherry or East Asian Cherry (more properly, really, since the tree originated in China), there can be no mistaking it in April when its serrated pink (or white) blossoms turn the tree into a huge pink (or white) ball, before showering the streets with the confetti of its petals a fortnight later. There are many varieties of Japanese Cherry, but three of the most common in Britain are 'Amanogawa' (pale pink double-layered flowers), 'Kanzan' (dark pink double-layered flowers) and 'Taihaku' (large white single-layered flowers).

Oriental Plane

London Plane (*Platanus x hispanica*)

A common city tree with two very distinctive features: its bark and its fruits. Look for grey-brown bark that flakes off to leave yellow patches; and football-like fruits that crash to the pavement below. The London Plane is a cross between the **Oriental Plane** (*Platanus orientalis*) and the **American Plane** (*Platanus occidentalis*).

Monkey Puzzle (*Araucaria araucaria*)

There's nothing in Britain like the Monkey Puzzle (or Chile Pine) with its miasma of shoots covered with dense, pointed cactus-like leaves and banana-shaped cones. It is also a rare example of a plant sometimes known by its Latin name (though only one of the two *Araucarias* is used).

Maidenhair Tree (*Ginkgo biloba*)

Maidenhair Tree

An extraordinary-looking tree that was introduced from China relatively recently but is known to have existed 200 million years ago, if fossil records are to be believed. Also known as a Ginkgo (Chinese for 'silver fruit'), the easiest way of identifying it is by its extremely unusual leaves that resemble Japanese fans with a cut in the middle.

EASY NATURE

Just remember this:

Any tree you see that you believe would puzzle a monkey is probably a Monkey Puzzle tree.

• The Japanese Cherry and its blossoms are known as *sakura* in Japan, where, aside from being a national symbol, they provide a metaphor for man's ephemeral existence.

What you should say:

'Sad to relate, but the poor old Maidenhair has no living relatives.'

No Frogs in our throats

Frog

A great many people receive their first lesson in biology standing by a primary school pond watching frogspawn turning into tadpoles turning into frogs. It is perhaps for this reason that the consumption of frogs has never taken off in Britain. However, having a life-cycle so profoundly swathed in memories of childhood masks the fact that frogs form a vital link in the food chain without which such diverse creatures as Herons, Hedgehogs, Foxes and Badgers, among others, would all go hungry. If you have a garden, attracting frogs to it is as simple as building a pond, which is also one of the most helpful actions anyone can take to help wildlife prosper.

Becoming a frog expert is a relatively simple affair on account of the very few species that live in Britain.

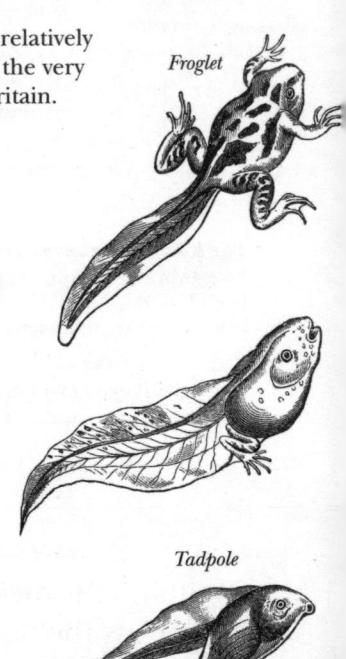

Froglet

Common Frog
(*Rana temporaria*)

Found everywhere but the remoter parts of Scottish islands, the olive-brown Common Frog (6–10cm) has a varying number of dark spots on its back and legs.

Marsh Frog (*Rana ridibunda*)

Slightly bigger (10–13cm) than the Common Frog but green all over (imagine a frog the way a child would paint it). An alien found only in certain small patches of south-east England.

Tadpole

Pool Frog (*Rana lessonae*)

The native species died out sometime at the end of the 20th century. Some alien Pool Frogs have been introduced haphazardly into isolated patches of southern England. A small frog (5–7 cm), it has a pale green stripe down its greeny-brown body and numerous dark spots.

European Tree Frog (*Hyla arborea*)

Since it adapts its colour to suit its environment, in the right circumstances this frog is almost neon green, as if coloured in with a lurid felt-tip pen. As its name suggests, it likes to live off the ground (though, alas, not always in trees). Another alien, those found in the wild have escaped from captivity.

EASY NATURE

Just remember this:

The most common frog
in Britain is called the
Common Frog.

- The **Edible Frog** (*Rana x esculenta*) – a Pool Frog/Marsh Frog hybrid with an unarguably unfortunate name – has been introduced into south and east England, where a few colonies thrive, unmolested by chefs.

- The **Agile Frog** (*Rana dalmatina*), though non-existent on mainland Britain, is the only frog found on Jersey.

What you should say:

'With no fur or feathers to pluck, the
ill-fated frog is the fast food of the food chain.'

Dismissed as a Newt

It might be their thundering great tails (that froglets and toadlets have the good breeding to absorb), or their slightly chubby bodies, but newts seem ever destined to be burdened with the tag of 'second-class lizards'. This is unjust because they are fascinating amphibians, equally at home on land or in water, and the courtship ritual of the Palmate Newt is something to behold.

Smooth Newts

The three British newts

Smooth Newt (*Triturus vulgaris*)

Also known as the Common Newt, the male Smooth Newt is yellow-brown with darkish spots (the female has smaller spots). However, in the breeding season (March/April), the male displays well-defined blotches and a crest from the back of its neck to the tip of its tail, and back underneath to its body again. His underside also turns an alarming orange. *Length:* To 10cm.

Palmate Newt (*Triturus helveticus*)

With very similar markings to the slightly larger Smooth Newt (look for the Palmate's unspotted throat), the male is best seen in the spring, when its feet become webbed (or 'palmate') and the tail ends in a sort of needle. Adult females are bright yellow with tiny small dark spots. *Length:* To 9cm.

Great Crested Newt (*Triturus cristatus*)

Britain's largest newt is darker than its cousins, and in the spring the male develops an unmissable saw-toothed crest down the length of its back. Mainly nocturnal and often spending long periods at the bottom of ponds, the Great Crested Newt is notoriously difficult to observe in the wild. *Length:* To 16cm.

The newt's pond quandary

Newts are seldom seen in the same ponds as fish because too many of their eggs get eaten (they have no compunction about eating the eggs and tadpoles of other amphibians themselves, though). They also prefer ponds that do not dry out in summer, so finding one large enough to remain wet, yet small enough not to be filled with fish, is often tricky.

A newt's year

April to August – born in a pond, becomes a tadpole and finally a juvenile newt (parents leave in early July).

September and October – leaves the pond, stalks about on land.

November to February – hides, falls into state of semi-hibernation.

March and April – returns to pond to breed (females lay around 200 eggs).

EASY NATURE

Just remember this:

All three are protected species under Schedule 5 of the Wildlife and Countryside Act 1981 (for maximum effect, always include 'Schedule 5' when mentioning this).

What you should say:

'The Palmate Newt is called *Triturus helveticus* after Triton, a Greek god of the sea, and Switzerland (Helvetia), the land-locked country where the species was first discovered, which is a pleasing irony really, isn't it?'

Toads and toadishness

The toad is too often considered the ugly cousin of the frog. However, anyone who has seen a tiny Common Toad toadlet (they're less than 1cm long) cannot but be moved by its dainty beauty. Since there are only two toad species found in any numbers in Britain – the Common Toad and the Natterjack Toad – identification is also pretty straightforward.

When to look

Unlike frogs, toads spend comparatively little time around water. Once they have grown big enough to leave their spawning pond, toads will return only to breed. Therefore, the best time to stake out a likely pond is March/April, when mating is often done in broad daylight (toads are otherwise largely nocturnal). The process of metamorphosis from egg to toadlet takes until about August. Outside of this period, toads can wander a mile or more from their pond.

Native toads

Common Toad (*Bufo bufo*)

By far Britain's most numerous and widespread toad, it can be identified by its olive-brown colouring, short hops and duck-like call (female 7–9cm; male 5–7cm).

Natterjack Toad (*Bufo calamita*)

Look for a diagnostic pale yellow line down the length of its body. The Natterjack (6–7cm) is a protected species famed for its digging ability which allows it to bury itself in seconds if alarmed.

Toad myths

Toads are not 'big frogs', as is too frequently supposed. Leaving aside the fact that they are from a completely different family (frogs being Ranidae, toads Bufonidae), the Common Toad (particularly the male of the species) is usually *smaller* than the Common Frog (see p. 174).

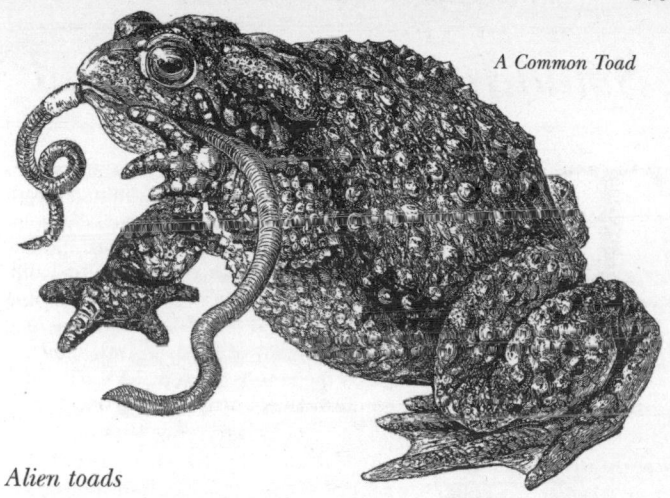

A Common Toad

Alien toads

Three toads have been introduced by accident or design and have established small communities. The dull grey **Midwife Toad** (*Alytes obstetricans*) is so called because the male (4–5cm) carries eggs around on his hind quarters until the tadpoles are ready to hatch. The **American Bullfrog** (*Bufo americana*) is huge (15–20cm) and capable of amphibian genocide in the wild. Finally there's the **African Clawed Toad** (*Xenopus laevis*), an exclusively aquatic, beady-eyed, yellow-brown creature (10–12cm).

EASY NATURE

Just remember this:

If you see what you think is a frog walking, you can be pretty sure it's a Natterjack Toad.

- Common Toads were once thought poisonous to eat. In reality, they're merely very unpleasant. Even fish, who are very partial to frog tadpoles, refuse to eat toad tadpoles.

- Female Common Toads can lay up to 5,000 toadspawn eggs at a time.

What you should say:

'The female toad can be accidentally suffocated by the writhing mass of males trying to mate with her. It's not a perfect world, is it?'

Small fish in a small pond

There are few things more charming than a small pond in a glade or a glassy brook adding its tinkling undercurrent to the sounds of the countryside. Of course, where there is water, there is life, and where there are small amounts of water, there are small creatures to enjoy it (notwithstanding a visit from a Heron (p. 146)). In such places thrive fish that might otherwise be eaten by their larger brethren in more substantial bodies of water. There follows a selection of small fish you might expect to find in bijou settings. Note that the length given is the usual range for an adult, but that long-lived individuals may grow somewhat larger.

A Stickleback

Three-spined Stickleback (*Gasterosteus aculeatus*)

Otherwise known as the Tiddler or the Tittlebat, the Three-spined Stickleback does what it says on the tin – it has three spines in a row on its back. It also has large eyes and a longish fin between the spines and the tail, with a corresponding one underneath. The male is green on top and red below with dabs of blue at the head and under the tail. The female is green with a very pale green underside. *Length:* 4–8cm.

Nine-spined Stickleback (*Pungitius pungitius*)

Irritatingly, the Nine-spined Stickleback can have anything from seven to twelve spines on its back. More stretched-looking but usually shorter than the Three-spined Stickleback, the male is green, while the female is green on top and yellow underneath. *Length:* 5–7cm.

Common Minnow (*Phoxinus phoxinus*)

A member of the carp family and a very slow-moving fish, the grey-green Minnow is unremarkable to look at. During the spawning season (May to July), the male does at least sport a red belly. At other times, the sexes are similar – look for black blotches down the back that appear to form a series of irregular 'V' shapes. *Length:* 6–10cm.

Common Gudgeon (*Gobio gobio*)

Another carp family member, the Common Gudgeon lives on the beds of streams. It has two barbels (long fleshy growths) hanging from its mouth and is metallic green on top with an off-white belly. *Length:* 10–15cm.

EASY NATURE

Just remember this:

The male Stickleback builds a nest
into which the female lays her eggs.

• In 1990, the Three-spined Stickleback featured on a Belgian 14-franc postage stamp. And people say that Belgium is a boring country.

What you should say:

'In February 1859, a shower of Minnows
and Sticklebacks fell on the Wedgwood
China Works at the village of Mountain
Ash in Glamorgan. That's why the Welsh
always carry an umbrella.'

Bigger fish to fry

I t is true to say that, if you are not an angler, there are very few occasions on which you will be called upon to identify a fish swimming along some river or stream. Furthermore, even in clear water, one fish tends to look much like another so, if circumstances do require you to put a name to the individual in the depths below, the odds are you will get it wrong. You are therefore on safer territory if you get to know just a small handful of commonplace but singular river-dwelling fish, and then you can at least rule these out of your enquiries. If you can then move the conversation on to the extraordinary life-cycle of the European Eel, there's a good chance everyone will have forgotten about the fish even before you mention the vast spawning grounds of the wide Sargasso Sea.

Some freshwater fish you should know

Rainbow Trout (*Oncorhynchus mykiss*)

Look for: Rainbowesque colouring: yellowy-green on top, a pink horizontal stripe down each side and blue on the bottom.

Adult Size: 25–45cm.

A Common Bream

Common Bream (*Abramis brama*)

Look for: A yellow body whose outline closely resembles NASA's Super Guppy transport plane. Dark fins.

Adult size: 30–50cm.

Other considerations: Found only in England.

Common Carp (*Cyprinus carpio*)

Look for: A yellow fish with a long fin down its back and two whiskers drooping either side of its mouth like the ends of an unruly moustache.

Adult size: 25–75cm.

Other considerations: The only other whiskered fish you are likely to encounter in British rivers are various species of **Catfish**, the **Barbel** (*Barbus barbus*) and the **Gudgeon** (*Gobio gobio*), none of which are yellow.

Northern Pike (*Esox lucius*)

Look for: A yellowy-green fish, often of gargantuan proportions, with a huge mouth and fearsome teeth. Eats more or less anything, including other Pike.

Adult size: 30cm–1.2m (although elderly specimens can grow to 1.5m).

The extraordinary life-cycle of the European Eel (*Anguilla anguilla*)

i. Spawns in the Sargasso Sea (a region in the mid-North Atlantic).

ii. Spends a year as a larva drifting along the Gulf Stream towards Europe, where it becomes a glass eel.

iii. Swims up a European river as an elver.

iv. Passes between ten and fourteen years as a yellow eel, finally maturing as a silver eel.

v. Migrates back to the Sargasso Sea to spawn and die.

EASY NATURE

Just remember this:

If you see a fish leaping upstream, particularly in Scotland, it is an **Atlantic Salmon** (*Salmo salar*).

What you should say:

'There's an extraordinarily high mortality rate among fish, so it's a rare one that dies of old age. Now, as I was saying about the European Eel …'

All you can eat

Thankfully, very few of us will ever find ourselves at such a point of hunger that we shall need to rely on wild food in order to survive. However, foraging for food has a long and noble tradition in Britain as a means of supplementing the basic diet, and there is a wonderful sense of simplicity gained from eating the occasional wild food snack in a world in which our lives are beset by ever-increasing complexity. While most people have picked blackberries (the fruit of the **Bramble** (*Rubus fruticosus agg.*)) as children, or even the odd **Wild Strawberry** (*Fragaria vesca*), the experiment has tended to die there. This is a missed opportunity, because the initiated will know that there are scores of common plants to be sampled. There are almost as many books on the subject as there are edible wild flora, with the naturalist Richard Mabey widely considered the king of the genre. However, unless you have set your heart on going feral and living off the land, a little basic knowledge will suffice.

Three wild plants traditionally harvested for food

Elder (*Sambucus nigra*)

The Elder is widespread throughout Britain, and handily its buds, flowers and berries all serve as victuals. The buds can be used as a salad ingredient. The flowers, which are unmistakeable in the late spring because they turn the whole shrub white, can be cut in whole clusters and used to make a cordial, or fried in batter and served with sugar and mint. Those flowers that are not harvested mature into clumps of black, round berries that make a very acceptable filling for pies or puddings when mixed with other autumn fruits. In

Elder

cities, picking elderberries will do everyone a favour because they will otherwise be eaten by pigeons (p. 132), which then turn all below them pink with their droppings.

When to harvest: buds – March; flowers – April–May; berries – August–October.

Purple Laver (*Porphyra umbilicalis*)

Although common on the shores of Britain, it is only the good people of Pembrokeshire who have seen fit to harvest and eat Laver in any quantity, usually as *bara lawr* (laverbread), a puréed form of the seaweed. Easily recognised by its wide (8cm) yet very thin fronds which lie about on rocks and beaches turning from green to purple.
When to harvest: All year.

Hawthorn (*Crataegus monogyna*)

Owing to its once-widespread use as a basic food source in the countryside, the Hawthorn is also known as the 'bread-and-cheese' tree. The leaf buds and young leaves have a sweet nutty flavour and can either be eaten on their own or added to salads (as can the flower buds), and go very well with a hard cheese. The familiar red berries (known as *haws*) make an excellent jelly when simmered with a crab apple or two and some sugar. For help in identifying the Hawthorn, see p. 168.
When to harvest: leaf buds – March–April; leaves – April–May; berries – September–October.

See also recipes for nettle soup (p. 83) and chestnut purée (p. 163), and advice on picking wild fungi (p. 203).

EASY NATURE

Just remember this:

The most delicious pudding known to humankind is blackberry fool. Simply pick some blackberries and purée them; whisk some evaporated milk until stiff (the milk, not you); add the puréed blackberries and whisk some more.

- Sloe gin can be made by adding sugar and *sloes* – the fruit of the **Blackthorn** (see p. 168) – to gin and leaving in sealed bottles for a couple of months, shaking occasionally to dissolve the sugar.

What you should say:

'Contrary to received wisdom, there is such a thing as a free lunch.'

Animals that turn
white in winter

Britain has just three animals that go white in winter, so it is well worth committing them to memory. They are the Ptarmigan, the Mountain Hare, and the Stoat. As you might expect, they change their appearance in order to camouflage themselves in snowy conditions, so it is no surprise that they all do this in Scotland, the snowiest region of Britain.

Ptarmigan (*Lagopus mutus*)

No one is sure exactly when this member of the grouse family inherited the silent p that transformed the Scottish Gaelic *tàrmachan* ('white one of the mountain') into something more Greek-looking. However, there is no doubting its favourite spot – the rugged Cairngorms – where the clever bird camouflages itself in summer too, its mottled grey plumage making it look like a rock. This is just as well, because it spends a lot of time on the exposed mountainside and is thus vulnerable to predators like the Golden Eagle (p. 139). The Ptarmigan moults in autumn, revealing snowy white plumage ready for the snows, its only blemish being a stubbornly black tail. The Polar Bear covers up its black nose with a white paw but the Ptarmigan cannot hide its tail in flight, and this undoubtedly gives you your best chance of spotting one.

Mountain Hare (*Lepus timidus*)

Even in summer, the Mountain Hare (or Blue Hare) is easily differentiated from the Brown Hare (p. 40) by its much shorter ears and stubbier body. Like Ptarmigans, however, it has an Achilles heel when turning white, in that its nose and the tips of its ears remain a dull fawn colour. Usually solitary creatures, Mountain Hares spend their days crouched in depressions behind rocks or Heather (p. 77), a plant whose young shoots they consume. They are thus best seen at dawn or dusk when they feed.

Stoat (*Mustela erminea*)

The great advantage to the armchair naturalist of the blanching of the Stoat in winter is that any Stoat-like creature that is white must *be* a Stoat and not, say, a Weasel or any other of its look-alike relatives (see pp. 34–5 for details of the potential confusion).

A Ptarmigan

EASY NATURE

Just remember this:

Paler than the mountain air
Are Ptarmigan, Stoat and Mountain Hare;
Purer than ere the fall of man
Are Mountain Hare, Stoat and Ptarmigan.

MORE EASY NATURE

Remember this too:

The Mountain Hare's Latin name, *Lepus timidus*, can be called to mind by imagining it *Leaping timidly* away from you as you stalk the Highlands.

What you should say:

'Another 30 years of global warming and they'll feel pretty silly turning white, those three.'

At the seaside

A day by the sea can be a great adventure for the naturalist, given the very different environments all within close proximity.

A Limpet

On the rocks

The mighty **Dogwhelk** (*Nucella lapillus*) mollusc may be seen biting through the shells of Mussels and sucking out their innards. Usually a dingy grey or white, it is physically similar to the Common Northern Whelk (see illustration on p. 214). Unsurprisingly, the empty shells of the **Common Blue Mussel** (*Mytilus edulis*) are often just as numerous on the beach as occupied ones on the rocks, although Mussels can sometimes defend themselves by tying Dogwhelks down with secreted *byssus* threads and starving them to death. Meanwhile, the **Common European Limpet** (*Patella vulgata*) must always return to the same niche on its rock, which its shell fits exactly, or it will dry out and die when the tide goes out.

On the sandy beach

Among the usual shells (p. 214) and man-made debris, there are often thousands of **Lugworms** (*Arenicola marina*), their presence given away by the familiar little casts – bundles of sand resembling tiny portions of spaghetti – that the Lugworm ejects from its burrow. Much like Earthworms in size and shape, they are reddish, fading to a yellow at the tail. Above them there may be **Bladder Wrack** (*Fucus vesiculosus*), a seaweed that first provided humans with iodine, and whose tiny airbags are a cunning flotation device.

Rock-pool life

A sandy pool on a rocky shoreline may harbour the **Common Goby** (*Pomatoschistus microps*), a tiny sandy-coloured fish (3–6cm) with two dorsal fins. Its larger (8–10cm) and equally well-camouflaged cousin, the **Sand Goby** (*Pomatoschistus*

minutus), often lurks in pools near
the low tide mark. Males
usually have a dark blue
spot at the rear of the first
dorsal fin. Larger still
(12–16cm), the attractive
Shanny (*Lipophrys pholis*) is
another rock-pool dweller,
and can also sometimes be
found awaiting high tide
among seaweed or
under damp
stones. Although
its colour
changes to suit its
surroundings, it
can usually be identified
by a red spot on its one
long dorsal fin and its
slimy scaleless skin. As a
rule, the best month to
investigate rock pools is
August.

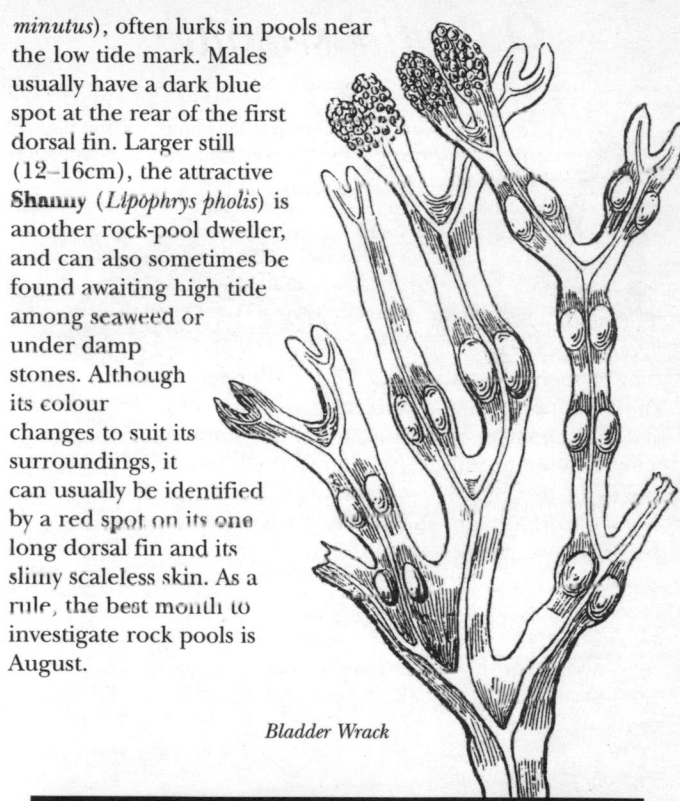

Bladder Wrack

EASY NATURE

Just remember this:

The commonest crab on our *shores* is the **Shore Crab**
(*Carcinus maenas*). A full-grown adult has a carapace
(shell) of around 6cm by 9cm and five small teeth on
the rim behind each eye. Its colour can be red,
brown, grey or green depending on its environment.

What you should say:

'That sucking sound you can hear is not me
eating my ice lolly but the Limpets tightening
their grip on the rock as we approach.'

Out of the mouths of babes and sucklings

I t can be quite upsetting to overhear an otherwise perfectly well-educated man or woman flap painfully about in the realms of unknowing on being asked by a child the proper name to call a certain baby creature. Dogs and cats with their puppies and kittens are simple enough, but when it comes to, say, hares, pigeons or dolphins, most people find themselves on shakier ground.

There follows a handy list of offspring names to memorise so that you too are not caught out at some future date.

Badger = Cub

Cow/Bull = Calf

Deer = Fawn

Dolphin = Calf

Duck = Duckling

Eagle = Eaglet

Eel = Elver

Ferret = Kit

Fox = Cub

Frog = Froglet

Goat = Kid

Goose = Gosling

Hare = Leveret

Hedgehog = Hoglet

Hen = Pullet

Horse = Foal

Otter = Cub

Owl = Owlet

Pig = Piglet

Pigeon = Squab

Rabbit = Kit or Kitten

Rat = Kitten or Pup

Seal = Pup

Sheep = Lamb

Swan = Cygnet

Whale = Calf

EASY NATURE

Just remember this:
Indiscriminately adding the suffix '–let'
onto the names of animals might get you
by for a while, but few people will be fooled
by 'Goatlet', 'Horselet' or 'Dolphinlet'.

• An adult Rabbit used to be known as a Coney (pronounced 'cunny'), while its offspring were called Rabbits.
However, by the 1800s, the word had been hijacked as a
euphemistic sound-alike for a term considered extremely
insulting, so Coney was quietly dropped in favour of
Rabbit. The King James Bible uses the word Coney, so
19th-century clergy avoided the possibility of titters in the
pews by altering the pronunciation so that it rhymed with
'pony'.

What you should say:
'Oh, that one's not a baby –
I'd say he's just a short adult.'

Burning wood

E very naturalist should know at least one poem that can be brought out on suitable occasions, such as when seated around a bonfire. The following anonymous ditty, while not overburdened with literary merit, is at least useful and appropriate.

Logs to burn, logs to burn
Logs to save the coal a turn
Here's a word to make you wise
When you hear the woodman's cries

Never heed his usual tale
That he has good logs for sale
But read these lines and really learn
The proper kind of logs to burn

Beechwood fires burn bright and clear
Hornbeam blazes too
If the logs are kept a year
And seasoned through and through

Oak logs will warm you well
If they're old and dry
Larch logs of pinewood smell
But the sparks will fly

Pine is good and so is **Yew**
For warmth through wintry days
But **Poplar** and **Willow** too
Take long to dry and blaze

Birch logs will burn too fast
Alder scarce at all
Chestnut logs are good to last
If cut in the fall

Holly logs burn like wax
You should burn them green
Elm logs like smouldering flax
No flame to be seen

Pear logs and **Apple** logs
They will scent your room
Cherry logs across the dogs[1]
Smell like flowers in bloom

But **Ash** logs, all smooth and grey,
Burn them green or old
Buy up all that come your way;
They're worth their weight in gold.

What you should say:
'Of course, you shouldn't burn
them at all in smokeless zones.'

---

[1] A reference to fire dogs (partially burnt wood), not dogs.

A compilation of collective nouns

One of the many attributes that separate the naturalist from the tiro is a thorough knowledge of the correct words to describe groups of animals. A man might very well point at some sheep and correctly identify them, but if, in doing so, he says, 'Look! Rare Lincoln Longwools! I've never seen such a large *pack*', he will find that his prowess with woolly ungulates will be swiftly drowned in a sea of derision at his failure to use the term 'flock'. Likewise, a woman referring to 'a *pride* of goats' will be laughed to scorn, even by people she believed to be her closest friends. It is thus a prerequisite to joining the ranks of the proper naturalist that you have a grasp of at least a dozen or so of the commoner group names for use when you venture out into the fields.

Some history

Collective nouns (group names) trace their origins back to the 15th century, and possibly earlier, when the hunting fraternity delighted in giving names to the groups of animals they despatched. Since the hunting of prey was called *venery*, such collective nouns were called *terms of venery*. Although most of the names have since evolved or changed completely over the years, the tradition of inventing terms for groups of animals lives on.

A warning

It has long been a pastime of intellectuals and other ne'er-do-wells to coin collective nouns that have no currency other than their value as humorous quips. While it might be entertaining to get some of these off pat in order to amuse your friends – 'an *aarmy* of aardvarks' or 'a repetition of parrots' are just two examples – they should not be treated as bona fide group names.

A rule of thumb would be that the more obviously witty a collective noun is, the less likely it is that it's been adopted by the naturalist community (even though they enjoy a good joke as much as the next person). Furthermore, since many of the non-humorous group names are also matters of dispute among naturalists, it's probably a good idea not to take too fundamentalist an approach to the subject.

Some basic collective nouns

A *brood* of Hens

A *colony* of Ants, Bats or Rabbits

A *drove* or *herd* of Pigs or Cattle

A *flock* of Sheep or Birds

A *school* or *shoal* of Fish

A *swarm* of Bees

EASY NATURE

Just remember this:

If in doubt, you can always sidestep the issue completely by referring to any concentration of animals as simply 'a group'.

Some more advanced examples

A *bed* of Oysters

A *boogle* of Weasels

A *cete* of Badgers

An *exaltation* of Skylarks

A *farrow* of Piglets

A *labour* of Moles

A *murder* of Crows

A *parliament* of Owls

A *pod* of Dolphins, Porpoises or Seals

A *romp* of Otters

A *skulk* of Foxes

A *smack* of Jellyfish

A *sounder* of Boars

A *string* of Ponies

A *trip* of Goats

Creatures that have spawned multiple collective nouns

Many animals, for good or ill, have inspired a plethora of group names, none of which have succeeded in ousting the others. With the exception of the ducks and geese, for whom there are specific terms for different states of being, you might want to learn just one of the names and stick with it.

Ducks: A *flock* (in flight), a *raft* (while floating on water) and a *paddling* (while swimming)

Frogs: an *army*, a *colony*, or a *knot*

Geese: a *gaggle* (on the ground), a *wedge* or *skein* (when flying in formation)

Ravens: a *conspiracy*, a *storytelling* or an *unkindness*

Rooks: a *building*, a *clamour* or a *parliament*

Toads: a *knob*, a *knot*, a *lump* or a *nest*

Whales: a *pod*, a *gam* or a *herd*

What you should say:

'Never confuse a knob of toads with a knob of butter, particularly when making toast.'

God's prescription service

The **Doctrine of Signatures** is a curious if strangely appealing philosophy based on the supposed similarities between certain sections of plants and parts of the human body (or animals or other inanimate objects), and the belief that the properties of the plant were linked in some healing way with the things they resembled. Thus the brain-like walnut was felt to be good for curing disorders of the brain. Although there are few people today (aside perhaps from certain homoeopathists and 'natural healers') who seriously subscribe to the doctrine, a basic knowledge of it does cast light on our civilisation's intriguing early stabs at 'doing medicine'.

Jakob Böhme's revelation

There were many early dabblings along similar lines to the Doctrine of Signatures going back to the ancient Greeks. Such ideas were given a boost in the post-medieval world by the Swiss physician and alchemist Paracelsus von Hohenheim (1490–1541), but the book that was to encapsulate the system and give a name to it didn't come along until Jakob Böhme (1575–1624) published *Signatura Rerum* (*The Signature of All Things*) in 1621. Böhme, a German shoemaker who lived outside the town of Görlitz, had a sort of a 'Eureka' moment in 1600 in which he saw that the relationship between God and humans was apparent in all things. However, it took another twelve years for him to write and arrange for the publication of his beliefs in a book entitled *Aurora*. The local council reacted by calling upon him not to write any further books on the subject. Böhme responded by moving to Prague to continue writing, and *Signatura Rerum* was (eventually) the result.

Böhme's philosophy becomes a doctrine

Böhme's *Signature of All Things* appealed to European Christians of a metaphysical persuasion, who set about expanding the ideas within its pages into a full-blown theology. They believed that God had designed every plant in such a way that each one was a lesson in theology if only people had eyes to see it. Their favourite example was the **Passionflower** (*Passiflora caerulea*), which was overflowing with signatures. The flower's corolla thus became a crown of thorns; the five petals and five sepals were the ten apostles (Judas the betrayer and Peter the denier being conveniently left out); the pistil stigmas were nails; the five stamens represented the wounds of Christ; the spots under the leaves were the pieces of silver given to Judas, etc., etc. In this way, careful study of any plant, no matter how simple, could determine what God had intended its purpose to be (and so give an insight into the mind of the Creator at the same time). All one had to do was examine a plant's 'signatures' – i.e. its overall outline; the shape of its constituent parts; the colour of its roots, stem, leaves and flowers; its natural habitat, etc.

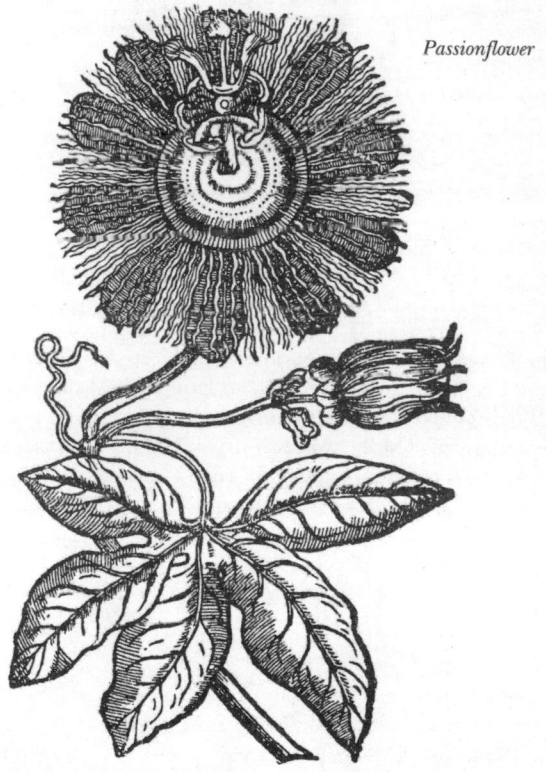

Passionflower

The well known English herbalist Nicholas Culpeper was a follower of the Doctrine of Signatures, and the system was discarded in mainstream medicine only as late as the 19th

God's prescription service *cont.*

century, when more exacting tests for discovering whether a particular plant had any curative properties (such as trial and error) became the norm.

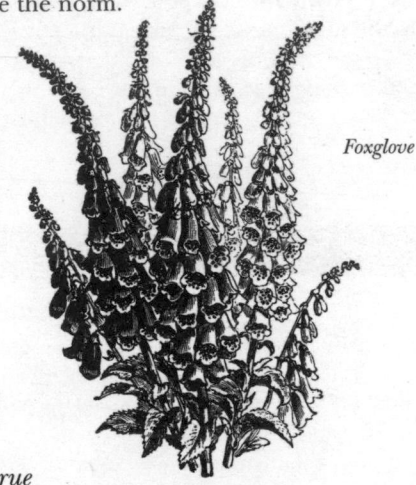

Foxglove

Strange but true

The **Foxglove** (*Digitalis purpurea*) bears strikingly heart-shaped fruit, making it a certainty that it can be used in the treatment of heart complaints, according to the precepts of the Doctrine of Signatures. Oddly, that has proved to be the case, since Foxgloves were the original source of *digitalis* (which is now synthetically produced), a drug used for various heart disorders.

St John's Wort

Liverwort

EASY NATURE

Just remember this:

In centuries past, many plants were named according to their apparent healing properties and topped off with *wort* (pronounced 'wurt'), from *wyrt*, the Old English word for 'plant' or 'herb'. Examples still around today include **Liverwort** (the *Hepatica* genus), **Feverwort** (the *Centaurium* genus) and **Lungwort** (the *Pulmonaria* genus).

• Long before Jakob Böhme was born, the Greek physician and 'father of medicine' Hippocrates (c. 460–c. 370 BC) had identified over 300 plants that he believed could be used to cure one illness or another.

What you should say:

'If *Fever*wort was meant to cure fevers, and *Liver*wort dealt with complaints of the liver, what sort of disease was *St John*?'[1]

---

[1]Just so that people realise you are making a wry comment about the vagaries of nomenclature, go on to explain that St John's Wort (*Hypericum perforatum*) was believed to be beneficial for skin complaints because of the tiny holes in its leaves which are a signature for the pores in human skin. Nowadays, it is more commonly known as a treatment for mild depression.

Really Fungi

Always remember that you are under no compulsion to eat fungi. Many people enjoy simply looking at them, identifying them, and moving on. Furthermore, if the mushrooms or toadstools happen to form a so-called 'fairy ring' (a perfectly acceptable term in the world of mycology), they bring a welcome air of mystique to the countryside.

What fungi do

In a nutshell, the purpose of a fungus is to produce sexual spores in order to reproduce itself. It survives long enough to do this by forming a *mycorrhizal* (mutually beneficial) relationship with a plant (typically a tree), or by breaking down dead material such as a fallen tree trunk, or by killing off the plant or creature it is living on and consuming it.

Some common fungi

Field Mushrooms

Field Mushroom (*Agaricus campestris*)

The wild cousin of the Cultivated Mushroom and very similar in appearance.

Status: Edible.

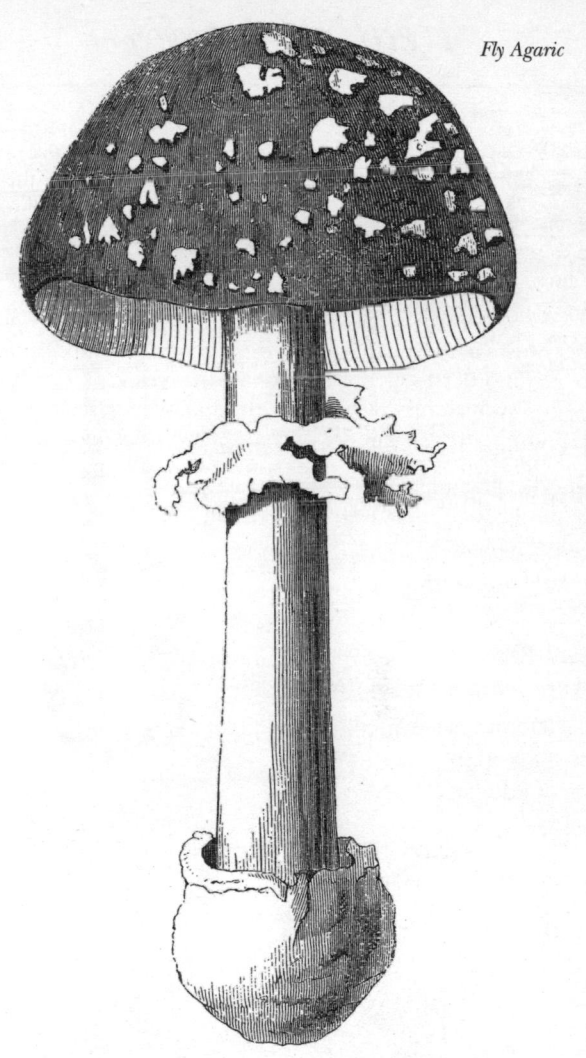

Fly Agaric

Fly Agaric (*Amanita muscaria*)

The Toadstool of everyone's imagination – with a red or orange cap and white spots, as used by gnomes the world over.

Status: Poisonous.

Really Fungi cont.

Death Cap
(*Amanita phalloides*)

Generally recognised to be the most poisonous fungus. It can take its unwary eater as little as six hours to die.

Status: Poisonous.

Death Cap

Destroying Angel (*Amanita virosa*)

Superficially similar to a clutch of edible mushrooms, the Destroying Angel is aptly named.

Status: Poisonous.

Jew's Ear
(*Auricularia auricula-judae*)

A gelatinous ear-shaped fungus often found on elm trees.

Status: Edible.

Common Puffball

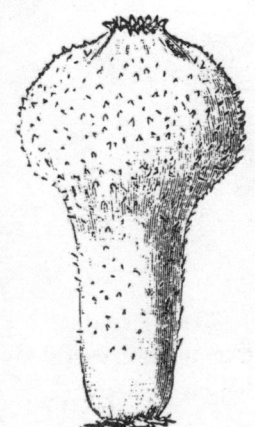

Common Puffball
(*Lycoperdon perlatum*)

Look for short spines surrounded by grainy scales. The spores puff out of the top on maturity.

Status: Edible (when young).

Eight rules to remember should you wish to eat wild fungi

i. Make absolutely certain that what you plan to eat is not only a non-poisonous species but an edible one, by making a positive identification of it using a field guide. If in any doubt at all, leave it alone.

ii. Do not pick old or decomposing specimens.

iii. Do not pick very wet fungi, they taste awful.

iv. Check all fungi for maggots.

v. Never harvest all the fungi you find in one particular spot, and never pick too much of something you've never tried before.

vi. To pick the fungus, twist it gently while pulling.

vii. Put your harvested fungi into an open basket – they will decay incredibly quickly inside pockets, plastic bags or Tupperware containers.

viii. Cook and eat as soon as possible after picking.

For more information on consuming the countryside, see *All you can eat* (p. 184).

EASY NATURE

Just remember this:
Of Britain's 3,000 or so large fungi, only around 20 are dangerously poisonous.

What you should **not** *say:*
'Why did everyone invite the mushroom to the party? Because he was a fun guy.'

How to date a hedgerow

Before you get too excited and imagine yourself being able to pin the planting of some gnarled row of ancient stunted Dogwood to a particular Tuesday in 1642, it should be stated that dating hedgerows by sight is a shockingly imprecise science. It is therefore a good idea to set your expectations low before you start out, and content yourself with the knowledge that, with a little practice, you might be able to tell the *approximate* age of a hedge, at least to the nearest couple of centuries. Of course, if you are attempting to impress certain others who might be accompanying you on a country walk, there is no reason to imagine that they are not also labouring under the illusion that hedge-dating methods are as accurate as the atomic clock, thus leaving you open to the temptation of claiming a little more confidence in the exactitude of your dating than the technique allows for. By all means feel free to put on a good performance, but do try to draw back from deducing the particular hour in the afternoon at which the final tree in the hedge was planted.

Some useful English history

The first Enclosure Act, which allowed for the enclosing of open fields – and the consequent denial to the 'common' people of the right to graze animals on them – was enacted by Parliament in 1604 (and concerned land in Radipole, Dorset). The zenith of such enclosures occurred between 1750 and 1850, when nearly 21 per cent of land in England (almost 7 million acres) was taken out of circulation. It has been estimated that roughly 200,000 miles of hedgerow were planted as a result. This means that a great many apparently ancient hedges are in fact no more than 150–250 years old. The key to identifying these 'Enclosure' hedges is their extreme straightness. The surveyors who divided up England did so with a ruler and set square, often taking no heed whatsoever of existing irregular field boundaries or geological features. Also note that Wales, Scotland and much of south-east England were spared the depredations of the Enclosures.

Hooper's Rule

Developed by Dr Max Hooper, E. Pollard and N.W. Moore and explained in their groundbreaking 1974 book *Hedges*, this is the only rule so far developed for dating hedgerows by sight:

Hedge age = (number of species in a 30-yard stretch) x 110 + 30 years

Therefore, if you find three different species, the hedge is 3 x 110 + 30 = 360 years old.

This works very well for some hedges, but unfortunately was proved to be hopelessly wrong for many others. When this was pointed out to him, Hooper hastily introduced a margin of error of plus or minus 200 years, making your 360-year-old hedge anything between 160 and 560.

Documentary evidence

It must be said that old maps, surveys, parish records and other relevant documents such as estate accounts remain far and away the best indicators of a hedge's true age. Even then, these must be tested out by work in the field, for it is quite possible for an ancient hedge to have died or been grubbed up and replaced by a much more modern one. This means that a combination of research in the archives and some examination of the hedge along the lines of Hooper's Rule is the most secure method of coming to a reasonable conclusion with regards to the age of a hedge.

Typical hedging trees

You can expect to come across all sorts of trees in hedges, but some of the more popular ones are Hawthorn (the over-whelming favourite), Ash, Elder, Hazel, Blackthorn, Maple, Wild Privet, Oak, Spindle, Crab Apple and Midland Hawthorn.

EASY NATURE

Just remember this:
When dating hedges, it's best to sit on the fence.

What you should say:

'The only sure way to date a hedgerow
is to get its phone number first.'

Endangered species

A ny naturalist worth his or her salt should have something worthwhile to say about endangered species. The names to drop in this context are the **EDGE List** (of which more later) and the **IUCN Red List of Threatened Species** (usually just called the IUCN Red List). The latter has been compiled by the International Union for the Conservation of Nature and Natural Resources since 1963 and is the most comprehensive assessment of the risk of extinction faced by plants and animals. The aim of the Red List is to draw the attention of both governments and the public to the plight of these species in order that some at least might be saved.

How it works

A species is classified according to various criteria, including the size of population, the number of locations in which it is found, the rate of decline, and how fragmented the species is (for example, a species with a population of 1,000 in one place could well have a greater chance of survival than one which has twenty separated groups of 50 – unless, of course, that one habitat is under threat). Each species is re-evaluated every five years, where possible.

The IUCN Categories

Each species is placed in one of seven categories according to the degree of danger of extinction in which it finds itself. The eighth category is reserved for those species for which there is insufficient information; while the ninth is for those that have yet to be assessed.

Extinct (EX)

Extinct in the Wild (EW)

Critically Endangered (CR)

Endangered (EN)

Vulnerable (VU)

Near Threatened (NT)

Least Concern (LC)

Data Deficient (DD)

Not Evaluated (NE)

Three endangered species in Britain

According to the IUCN Red List, the only Critically Endangered (CR) terrestrial animal in Britain is the visiting **Sociable Lapwing** (*Vanellus gregarius*). The reasons for its rapid recent decline are unclear, which sadly makes its conservation all the more difficult. There are two fish off the coast of Britain that are also Critically Endangered. The **Blue Skate** (*Dipturus batis*) – which, for the moment, is Europe's largest skate – has been fished almost into extinction. Its large body means that even very large-mesh nets will catch it. The **Angel Shark** (*Squatina squatina*) was once common in the north-east Atlantic but, being a frequent bycatch, its numbers have dwindled rapidly in the last half-century. It has already been declared extinct in the North Sea.

EASY NATURE

Just remember this:

When discussing the IUCN Red List, the term 'threatened' officially refers to the three categories: *Critically Endangered*, *Endangered*, and *Vulnerable*.

The EDGE List

• The Zoological Society of London (ZSL) compiles the EDGE List (Evolutionarily Distinct and Globally Endangered). As the title suggests, each species on the list is ranked according to whether there is anything out there similar to it, and how threatened with extinction it is.

• Tragically, there is little or no work being done to preserve 75 per cent of the species found on the EDGE List's 'Top 100'. A case in point is the No. 1 on the list, the **Yangtze River Dolphin** (*Lipotes vexillifer*), which may already have become extinct because calls to conserve it went unheeded.

• To date, ZSL has ranked only mammals, but there are plans to expand the list into other areas.

What you should say:

'I notice the plucky little Harbour Porpoise isn't doing all that well either.'[1]

---

[1] The **Harbour Porpoise** (*Phocoena phocoena*) is classified as Vulnerable (VU).

Carolus Linnaeus
(1707–78)

Even if you're not a historian, you should know something about Carolus Linnaeus, for it was he who gave the world the system by which all living things are classified. If that sounds rather dull, it shouldn't, for without Linnaeus, the world would be a much more confusing place. Take the wild flower *Atropa belladonna* (p. 86), for example. One person may call it Deadly Nightshade, another knows it as the Devil's Cherries, while a third calls it a Dwayberry. It is only because of Linnaeus' central naming system that we can be sure that all three people are actually talking about the same plant.

Early life

Linnaeus was born on 23 May 1707 on a farm in the southern Swedish province of Småland. Although his parents hoped he would go into the Church, his facility for botany caught the attention of a local doctor who ensured that young Carl studied the subject at university. At the age of 25 he led an expedition to Lapland and published his findings as *The Florula Lapponica*. His career was up and running.

Failure

Frustrated that there was no universal system for classifying plants, Linnaeus hit upon what he called the *Sexual System*. This divided plants according to their sexual organs – the *stamens* and *pistils*. Fellow naturalists and churchmen were duly scandalised. German botanist Johann Siegesbeck attacked the system as 'loathsome harlotry – who would have thought that Bluebells, Lilies and Onions could be up to such immorality?' More importantly, perhaps, the system didn't work very well.

Success

However, the 'binomial' method that Linnaeus had developed to name the plants he was classifying was much more useful. It is now applied to all living things, which is how we came to be known as *Homo sapiens* (see p. 210).

Happy ending

Linnaeus married in 1739 and had seven children. He was ennobled in 1761, taking the name Carl von Linné. He died in 1778 during a ceremony in Uppsala Cathedral.

EASY NATURE

Just remember this:

Linnaeus' most important work is *Systema Naturae* (*System of Nature*), whose tenth and definitive edition was published in 1758. In it he divides living things (and minerals too, just for good measure) by class, order, genus and species – terms we still use today.

- Linnaeus mis-spelt the Irish heather named after St Dabeoc as St Daboec's Heath (*Daboecia cantabrica*). The plant has been saddled with the error ever since.

- The first place in Britain to use the Linnaean system was the University of Oxford Botanic Garden.

- The first edition of Linnaeus' *Systema Naturae* (1735) consisted of eleven pages of species. By the thirteenth and final edition (1770) it had grown to 3,000 pages.

What you should say:

'"God created, Linnaeus set in order," if I may quote Johann Fabricius for a moment.'

Making the Linnaean System work for you

'I have fundamentally reorganised the whole field of Natural History, raising it to the height it has now attained. I doubt whether anyone today could hope, without my help and guidance, to make any advance in this field.'

So wrote the Swedish naturalist Carolus Linnaeus (p. 208), a man famous for enjoying no more than a passing acquaintance with the basic rudiments of humility. However, it has to be admitted that the reorganisation to which he was referring *was* impressive. The system upon which he settled for naming all living things is fundamentally the same one in use today, 250 years later, and bears the Swedish naturalist's name, a fact that would no doubt be a source of considerable pleasure to him. Therefore, anyone who wishes to get some sort of grasp on nature would do well to know what the Linnaean System is all about, even if, ever after, they think of a Robin as simply a Robin and not *Erithacus rubecula*.

The binomial name

Linnaeus' achievement was two-fold. First, he came up with a method by which any living thing could be given a two-word (*binomial*) name; and second, he produced a structure into which all living things – and, crucially, all future discoveries – could be placed, so that some order could be brought to the natural world in which we live.

The simplest way to look at the binomial naming scheme is to imagine it in the same way that Linnaeus himself did: as a surname (*genus* name) followed by a first name (*species* name). Thus, human beings are classified as:

Genus	Species
Homo	*sapiens*

To each species a place in the grand scheme of life

Linnaeus' second impressive accomplishment was the structure he established, making the ordered classification of all living things possible for the first time. After one or two early teething errors, his basic hierarchy became:

Kingdom / Phylum / Class / Order / Family / Genus / Species

Each one of these groups (kingdom, family, etc.) is called a *taxon* and there are now many many other taxons in the hierarchy, such as microphylum and infraclass, but these are of concern only to botanists and others who are paid to know them.

Using this structure, the full scientific name (shown in bold) for the European Rabbit (p. 40) is:

Taxon	Name	Rough meaning
Kingdom	**Animalia**	Multi-cellular, able to respond to environment, etc.
Phylum	**Chordata**	Possessing some sort of spinal cord
Class	**Mammalia**	Females produce milk for their offspring
Order	**Lagomorpha**	Possessing four incisor teeth in the upper jaw
Family	**Leporidae**	Being a Rabbit or a Hare
Genus	***Oryctolagus***	Being something that digs
Species	***cuniculus***	Being something that lives in tunnels

However, like all living things, the European Rabbit's genus/species name is unique, so rather than calling it *Animalia Chordata Mammalia Lagomorpha Leporidae Oryctolagus cuniculus,* it can simply be referred to as *Oryctolagus cuniculus.*

EASY NATURE

Just remember this:

Binomial (or scientific) names are always italicised, with the first letter capitalised and all the rest in lower case – so the binomial name for Heather is written *Calluna vulgaris.*

• The craft of according each species its rightful place in the structure is called *taxonomy.*

What you should say:

'There are only two things you can be certain about in life: death and taxons.'

[1]There are such things as sub-species, which bear three names, but there is no need to lose sleep over them (see p. 228).

Sterling Mosses

One of the most overlooked groups of living things is the mosses. This is doubtless because they rarely grow to any significant height, and never seem to do anything much. While this is true to a certain degree, the spongy moss world is a fascinating place on closer inspection. Indeed, in Victorian times, moss-collecting became something of a craze, with people building their own mosseries in which they cultivated mosses scavenged from the wild. Although one would hardly advocate such behaviour today, the collectors did at least recognise just how interesting mosses could prove to be if given the necessary attention.

How to tell that something is a moss and not just some other plant

i.   Mosses do not flower, so nothing with a flower can be a moss.

ii. Other plants have roots, mosses do not (they have tiny threads called *rhizoids*).

iii. Liverworts appear similar but are endowed with fleshy leaves called lobes.

iv. Lichens often grow in the same places but usually form a sort of crust.

Britain – a damp and temperate place

Mosses survive by extracting moisture from the air through their stems and rhizoids, which is why they can live on rocks and walls and other places where there is no soil. Therefore, the fact that Britain is a damp country suits them down to the ground. They are also not keen on the cold, so the island's relatively warm climate makes it doubly attractive, meaning that several hundred species have made it their home, and in doing so have made Britain the envy of many mossless countries whose climates are not so appealing. Unfortunately, many of those hundreds of species look frighteningly similar, so it might be best to see how you get on with two common mosses and go on from there.

Grey-cushioned Grimmia (*Grimmia pulvinata*)

One of a large family of the imposingly named Grimmiaceae, Grey-cushioned Grimmia is often found on walls or roofs. It is green rather than grey but it does form roughly circular cushions, about 3cm across. The grey in its name refers to the distinctive whitish hairs that stick out like grass from its pointed leaves.

Peat Moss (*Sphagnum genus*)

There are over 40 different species of Peat Moss (otherwise known as Bog Moss or Sphagnum). A common one is the **Blunt-leaved Bog Moss** (*Sphagnum palustre*) which has spirals of small, slightly spiky branches that can grow up to 25cm, making it one of the grander mosses.

EASY NATURE

Just remember this:

Peat Moss is often found in peat bogs. It is no surprise then that peat largely consists of decayed Peat Moss.

- When disinfectants ran short during the First World War, Peat Moss laced with lavender oil was used as a makeshift first-aid dressing on soldiers' wounds.

What you should say:

'For the record, liverworts also have rhizoids but they are uni-cellular and nothing like the complex multi-cellular rhizoids that mosses possess, and while we're about it, try not to confuse *those* liverworts, which comprise a whole division of plants called Marchantiophyta, with the completely separate buttercup family members of the same name.'

They shell have names

T he coastline of mainland Britain is 11,072.76 miles long and is home to untold millions of shells, so it seems not a little dismal that when the vast majority of the population of the island is faced with a shell, they can make no more incisive a declaration with regard to its identification or history than that it is 'a shell'. Make yourself part of the minority.

How a shell comes to be on a beach

The first thing to remember is that each empty shell once had a being inside it, and that being was a sea-living mollusc. At some point, after having developed from an egg to the larval stage, the mollusc secreted the material (mainly calcium carbonate) that became the hard coat that we call a shell. This newly housed mollusc is most likely to be a Gastropod or a Bivalve (a few are Chitons, Cephalopods or Tusks, but there's no need to concern yourself with them at this stage). After death, the soft-bodied creature decays (if it hasn't already been eaten), leaving an empty shell to be washed up on the shore. Eventually, the shell will be crushed by the tides to form sand, upon which yet more shells will be beached.

Gastropods

With a few exceptions, this class has tubular shells that look as though they have been coiled around an axle (except that no such axle ever existed). These are the classic 'put it to your ear and listen to the sea' shells.

A common Gastropod –
Common Northern Whelk (*Buccinum undatum*)

Bivalves

Occasionally you will find both halves
of a Bivalve shell, but more often
than not they will have come
apart. Most of these half shells,
if held with the inside pointing
upwards, look like miniature
outdoor auditoria. One notable
exception to this rule is the familiar **Giant Razor Shell** (*Ensis siliqua*),
which resembles a long canoe.

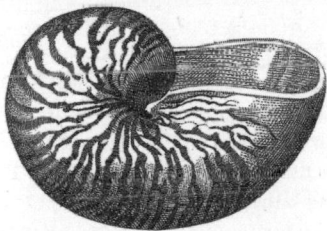

A common Bivalve –
Great Scallop
(*Pecten maximus*)

A Cephalopod (just so you know) –
Chambered Nautilus (*Nautilus pompilius*)

EASY NATURE

Just remember this:

Gastropod comes from the Latin meaning stomach-foot,
a reference to the fact that the mollusc within crawls
around on its stomach which is also, therefore, its 'foot'.

- Britain's coastline falls within the 'Boreal' zoogeographical
  province, which includes the north-east coast of North America,
  southern Iceland, and north-west Europe.

- The woman of whom it was said, 'She sells seashells on the sea
  shore', was Mary Anning – 19th-century palaeontologist, discoverer
  of huge marine dinosaurs, and seller of fossils (and shells) in the
  small Dorset resort of Lyme Regis.

What you should say:

'I'm not much of a conchologist, but
even I know the shell of the Griffith's
Turrid is found only in the Indo-Pacific.'

Slugs and sluggishness

V ery few people know the first thing about slugs, so even being able to reel off the names of a few common examples is viewed as something of an achievement, if rather an eccentric one. However, those who gently mock you are likely to be the first to admit surprise that slugs are not mere tubes of slime but are surprisingly similar to us, with their own heart, lung and kidneys, and are owed more respect as living creatures than we give them.

Three things about slugs with which you can surprise people

i. It's simply not true that they live off the vegetation lovingly grown in gardens. Unless it's the only thing around to eat, which is very rare since slugs have very catholic tastes (fungi, dung, carrion etc.), vegetables and flowers form but a very small portion of their diet.

ii. They have shells. Admittedly, on most slugs, they are internalised,[1] minuscule and offer no protection, but they are there nonetheless.

iii. They have been taken for many centuries as a remedy for a wide range of ailments including toothache and warts. Boiling a slug in milk and swallowing whole (or simply eating one alive) was also thought to be a good way of curing tuberculosis.

Three groups of slug you can name

Slugs are either **Keelback**, **Roundback** or **Shelled**. Keelbacks have a ridge (or 'keel') towards the hind end and a respiratory pore (called a *pneumostome*) on the right-hand side of its back. Roundbacks have no ridge, and the pore is nearer the head. Shelled slugs have exterior shells like snails (but there are not many of them).

Three types of slug you can name

The **European Black Slug** (*Arion ater*) is not always black (indeed, it can be white), but if you chance upon a slug that is around 10–15cm long, you are probably looking at a full-

---

[1] Although it's worth noting that the **Santa Barbara Shelled Slug** (*Binneya notabilis*) is one of a small band of slugs that *do* have an external shell.

grown adult. Another Roundback, the **European Red Slug** (*Arion rufus*), is very similar but, less confusingly, always red or brown. Smaller than its black cousin (usually to 10cm), it also has the pneumostome further away from its head. The **Great Grey Slug** (*Limax maximus*) is one of the largest Keelback slugs (to 20cm) and has a brown body with black spots, giving rise to its other names: Tiger Slug and, more appropriately, the Spotted-leopard Slug.

The trials of reproduction

Slugs are hermaphrodite (i.e. each individual is both male and female) and can fertilise themselves, although they prefer to team up with another slug. They do this by coiling their corkscrew penises around each other to exchange sperm. Unfortunately, they often become too tangled up to separate and the partners are forced to gnaw off each other's penis, a practice called *upophalla-tion*, and not one to be brought up over the dinner table. This makes both slugs involved effectively female, and they remain so ever after.

EASY NATURE

Just remember this:
The smoothish front part of a slug near the head is called a mantle, while the bit underneath that propels it forward is the foot.

• Slug predators include frogs, toads, Hedgehogs, snakes, ducks and Blackbirds.

What you should say:
'If you must wage war against the slugs in your garden, don't do so by pouring salt all over them, for this draws out all the moisture within, literally desiccating the poor things alive – a fate one wouldn't wish on one's worst enemy.'

Creepy crawlers

Snakes are creatures that have largely failed to worm their way into the hearts of the British people. How much of the public's distaste can be ascribed to the bad press the snake has received for its part in the temptation of Adam and Eve is difficult to say, but there is unarguably a persistent folk belief that snakes are nasty and unpleasant and, quite probably, evil. Perhaps if they were furry we would grow to love these largely harmless protected species a bit more.

Grass Snake (*Natrix natrix*)

Britain's largest and longest terrestrial reptile is best known for its ability to feign death, which it does by going completely limp with its mouth open and tongue hanging uselessly out. However, this astonishingly realistic performance is carried out only *in extremis* after the Grass Snake's first lines of defence – hissing, thrashing about violently, and squirting a malodorous fluid from its anal glands – have failed to thwart the attacker. Though once common throughout England and Wales, the Grass Snake has been in serious decline over the last few decades.

Length: To 1.2m.
Markings: Olive-green with dark vertical stripes down its sides; a black and yellow band at the neck; and off-white and black chequered undersides. Round pupils.
Hibernates: October to March.
Diet: Mainly frogs and toads.

Adder (*Vipera berus*)

Reports of humans being bitten by Adders are rare, and fatalities even more so: statistics kept between 1876 and 1976 record only fourteen Adder-related deaths. The Adder has taken to living as far from human disturbance as possible, usually where there is good cover and sufficient prey.

Length: To 65cm.
Markings: A 'V' on its head and a dark zigzagging line down the length of its back. Base colour can be anything from reddy-brown to yellow, grey, ivory or black (hence 'Black Adder'). Red eyes with vertical pupils.
Hibernates: October to March.
Diet: Small mammals, young birds, lizards.

Smooth Snake (*Coronella austriaca*)

This Heather-loving snake is in danger of disappearing altogether and can now be found only on dry sandy heaths in Dorset, the New Forest and Surrey. The Smooth Snake constricts its prey, in the manner of a Boa Constrictor, before consuming it alive and head-first.

Length: To 75cm.

Markings: Olive-green with a darker head and indistinct blotches down its back. Round pupils.

Hibernates: October to April.

Diet: Lizards, Slow Worms, insects.

A Grass Snake

EASY NATURE

Just remember this:

Often believed to be a snake, the Slow Worm (*Anguis fragilis*) is actually a legless lizard (p. 220).

What you should say:

'… Like the fellow who claimed he'd been poisoned by a Grass Snake bite – quite a feat, as I pointed out to him, seeing the creature has no fangs.'

Creepy crawlers *cont.*

The lizard is a reptile more often than not seen for an instant out of the corner of an eye as it makes for some dark nook at dizzying speed. Although associated more with sun-baked, siesta-drowsy Mediterranean villages than colder climes, there are three species of lizard native to mainland Britain.

Common Lizard (*Lacerta vivipara*)

Far and away the one you are most likely to encounter, the Common Lizard inhabits nearly the whole of Britain, and is absent only from pockets of the country such as parts of the Midlands and most Scottish islands. It is has a sludgy brown base colour with dark spots and a distinctive dark line running down the centre of its back.

Length (including tail): To 15cm.

Sand Lizard (*Lacerta agilis*)

A protected species and now, sadly, very rare. If you are lucky (and patient) and visit the heathlands of Hampshire, Dorset or Surrey, or the sand dunes of Merseyside, you might see one basking in the spring sun. The Sand Lizard is not sand-coloured but a dark olive-brown which, in the case of the male, changes in the breeding season (April/May) so that its head and flanks are a brilliant green which seems too gaudy to be natural. The female is slightly smaller and less showy, with a light-brown speckled body.

Length (including tail): To 20cm.

Slow Worm (*Anguis fragilis*)

A legless lizard (try to refrain from making the obvious joke if you can), the Slow Worm can easily be differentiated from any snake because it can close its eyelids. The Slow Worm comes in various shades of brown with bluey underparts. It often makes its home on railway embankments but is rarely seen in more urban settings due to the predations of the domestic cat.

Length: To 40cm.

Two exotic lizards

The **Wall Lizard** (*Podarcis muralis*) can be observed on its native Jersey, the Isle of Portland in Dorset, or beneath the cliffs on the Isle of Wight. It is very similar to the Common Lizard in looks, but a couple of centimetres longer, so take a ruler. The **Green Lizard** (*Lacerta viridis*), on the other hand, is unmistakable. Found on Jersey, Guernsey and the Isle of Wight, it is relatively large (to 40cm, including tail) and a bright speckled green all over.

A Green Lizard

• In a bid to maintain a population in Britain, the Sand Lizard has recently been reintroduced to sites in North Wales, Cornwall, Devon and Sussex.

What you should say:

'Unlikely, I know, but the Common Lizard's tail can be up to twice the length of its body.'

Eight legs good

There are two things that make a creature a spider: an ability to make a web out of a self-made silk thread, and a recognisable 'spidery' look (having eight legs helps). There are other areas, however, that allow for greater flexibility. For example, although most members of the Araneae order have eight eyes, some have six, four or two, and still others none at all. The female spider tends to be larger than the male (and in some famous cases, gets to eat him after mating), but even here there are some notable exceptions, such as the extraordinary Water Spider, which lives out most of its life under water in an air bubble kept in place by a silk submarine.

Common spiders that live in houses

House Spiders (*Tegenaria genus*)
There are five species of House Spider but the one you are most likely to encounter is the **Common House Spider** (*Tegenaria domestica*) which is also the smallest one (to 1cm). Look for their sheet webs (rather tangly affairs that lead to a tubular hidey-hole) in dark corners of rooms.

Daddy-Long-Legs Spiders (*Pholcus phalangioides*)
Imagine a Daddy-Long-Legs (p. 110) without the wings. The various species are prone to cannibalism.

Common spiders that live in gardens

Money Spiders
(Linyphiidae family)
Money Spiders are very small (usually much less than 1cm). The very common *Gonatium rubellum* is a marvellous bright orange colour.

Common Garden Spider
(*Araneus diadematus*)
Watch from June to November for nocturnally-spun orb webs

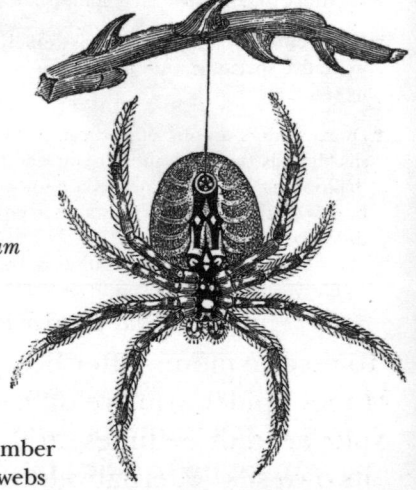

A Common Garden Spider

(the 'traditional' round web so beloved by the operators of ghost trains) containing a spider (up to 1.5cm) that could be black or, unhelpfully, almost any shade of brown or red.

Wolf Spiders (Lycosidae family)
So named after the mistaken belief that they hunt their prey in packs (they actually hunt solo), the browny-grey Wolf Spider is very probably the spider you've just seen running along the edge of a lawn or across a vegetable patch. The **Black-bellied Tarantula** (*Lycosa narbonnensis*) is also a Wolf Spider, but is unlikely to appear in a garden near you any time soon (unless you live in southern Italy).

Two easy spiders to spot

Funnel Web Spiders (Dipluridae family) are known for the funnel-shaped webs they build in the crevices of walls and rocks; while **Jumping Spiders** (Salticidae family) can jump.

EASY NATURE

Just remember this:

The organs in the spider's abdomen that *spin* the silk are called *spinnerets*.

- Contrary to popular belief, spiders are *not* insects but *arachnids*.

- Being bitten by a spider is an extremely rare event in Britain, and no native species can do more than inconvenience a human with its venom.

- Dwarf spiders, among others, can fly by letting the wind blow their silk threads (to which they are attached), an activity known as 'ballooning'. Spiders have been known to travel hundreds of miles by this method, and are thus able to colonise the remotest and tiniest of islands.

What you should say:

'To receive money after being alighted upon by a Money Spider, you are obliged to whirl it around your head three times on the end of a length of its own silk. Alternatively, you could get a job.'

The joy of Latin

Latin's a dead language,
As dead as dead can be.
First it killed the Romans,
Now it's killing me.

This slice of doggerel was once popular among children forced to study Latin at school, and the prospect of having to learn the language in order to give a plant or animal its 'proper' name (i.e. its *binomial* or scientific name – see p. 210) probably appeals just as much to the aspiring naturalist as it did to those pupils who had to tussle with the subject in order to pass exams. However, it should be pointed out that you can make Latin your friend rather than your persecutor. For example, the Latin labels given to living things may give a clue as to their appearance or habitat – information that might distinguish them from similar species, and something that common English names might well omit. Also, a goodly number of plants and creatures out there are known by a bewildering variety of nicknames in English, so knowing the scientific name is the only way to be sure that one man's **Marjoram** is indeed another woman's **Oregano** (they're both *Origanum vulgare*).

Clues to look out for in Latin names

Numbers

Species that are unusual in having two, three, four or more of some particular feature – or just the one of them, when all its cousins have two – may often have this mentioned in their binomial name.

1 = *mono-* or *uni-*
2 = *bi-*
3 = *tri-*
4 = *quad-* or *tetra-*
5 = *quin-* or *penta-*
6 = *sex-*
7 = *septem-*
8 = *oct-*
9 = *non-*
10 = *dec-*
12 = *dodec-*
Few = *olig-* or *pauci-*
Many = *poly-*

Habitats

If you know where something is usually found, you can save yourself the bother of looking for it in unlikely places. For example, there's little point in searching for **Thrift** up a mountain, since its binomial name, *Armeria maritima*, suggests you're more likely to find it in *maritime* situations – i.e. the coast.

aquatica = found in or near **water**
Reed Sweet Grass (*Glyceria aquatica*)
Water Spider (*Argyroneta aquatica*)

arborea = found in or resembling a **tree**
Tree Mallow (*Lavatera arborea*)
Woodlark (*Lullula arborea*)

arvens- = found in a **field**
Basil Thyme (*Acinos arvensis*)
Charlock (*Sinapis arvensis*)
Field Mouse-ear (*Cerastium arvense*)
Skylark (*Alauda arvensis*)

campestr- = found in a **field**
Field Maple (*Acer campestre*)
Field Mushroom (*Agaricus campestris*)
Green Tiger Beetle (*Cicindela campestris*)

pratens- = found in a **meadow**
Goatsbeard (*Tragopogon pratensis*)
Meadow Cranesbill (*Geranium pratense*)
Meadow Pipit (*Anthus pratensis*)

sylv- = found in a **wood**
Scots Pine (*Pinus sylvestris*)[1]
Wood Mouse (*Apodemus sylvaticus*)

[1]Most Scots Pines, being trees, are likely to be found in woods, so this is perhaps less helpful than it might be.

The joy of Latin *cont.*

Physical features

Some species are blessed with a characteristic that marks them out from their fellows. The Latin name will often reflect this.

cristat- = something with a **crest**
Crested Lark (*Galerida cristata*)
Great Crested Grebe (*Podiceps cristatus*)
Great Crested Newt (*Triturus cristatus*)

hirsut- = something **hirsute** (hairy)
Great Willowherb (*Epilobium hirsutum*)
Hairy Bitter-cress (*Cardamine hirsuta*)

minutus = something **minute**
Harvest Mouse (*Micromys minutus*)
Little Bittern (*Ixobrychus minutus*)
Sand Goby (*Pomatoschistus minutus*)

pseudo- = something that could be (or has been) **mistaken** for something else
Douglas Fir (*Pseudotsuga menziesii*)
Sycamore (*Acer pseudoplatanus*)

ruf- = something **reddish**
Red-legged Partridge (*Alectoris rufa*)
European Red Slug (*Arion rufus*)

Distribution

vulga- = something **common** (the original meaning of 'vulgar' in English)
Common Wasp (*Vespula vulgaris*)
European Limpet (*Patella vulgata*)
Heather (*Calluna vulgaris*)
Marjoram (*Origanum vulgare*)
Smooth Newt (*Triturus vulgaris*)
Wild Basil (*Clinopodium vulgare*)

Healing properties

> *officina-* = a plant identified in
> times past as having some medicinal purpose
> Common Scurvygrass (*Cochlearia officinalis*)
> Dandelion (*Taraxacum officinale*)
> Hedge Mustard (*Sisymbrium officinale*)
> Mouse-ear Hawkweed (*Pilosella officinarum*)

Easy Latin names to remember

If you wish to learn a few Latin names for species, the simplest
way to begin is by focusing on those whose genus and species
name are the same, since once you know one half, you've got
the whole thing. Here is a selection of common examples to
get you started.

Birds

> Buzzard (*Buteo buteo*)
> Common Crane (*Grus grus*)
> Corncrake (*Crex crex*)
> Bullfinch (*Pyrrhula pyrrhula*)
> Goldfinch (*Carduelis carduelis*)
> Hawfinch (*Coccothraustes coccothraustes*)
> Serin (*Serinus serinus*)
> Grey Partridge (*Perdix perdix*)
> Greylag Goose (*Anser anser*)
> Lapwing (*Vanellus vanellus*)
> Magpie (*Pica pica*)
> Manx Shearwater (*Puffinus puffinus*) – distressingly,
> this is *not* a Puffin
> Quail (*Coturnix coturnix*)
> Red Kite (*Milvus milvus*)
> Sand Martin (*Riparia riparia*)
> Shelduck (*Tadorna tadorna*)
> Swift (*Apus apus*)
> Whooper Swan (*Cygnus cygnus*)
> Willow Grouse (*Lagopus lagopus*)
> Wren (*Troglodytes troglodytes*)

The joy of Latin cont.

Mammals

Edible Dormouse (*Glis glis*)
Fallow Deer (*Dama dama*)
Fox (*Vulpes vulpes*)
Harbour Porpoise (*Phocoena phocoena*)
Otter (*Lutra lutra*)
Pipistrelle Bat (*Pipistrellus pipistrellus*)

Fish

Angel Shark (*Squatina squatina*)
Barbel (*Barbus barbus*)
Common Minnow (*Phoxinus phoxinus*)
European Eel (*Anguilla anguilla*)
Gudgeon (*Gobio gobio*)
Nine-spined Stickleback (*Pungitius pungitius*)
Stoneloach (*Barbatula barbatula*)

Others

Grass Snake (*Natrix natrix*)
Monkey Puzzle Tree (*Araucaria araucaria*)

Deeply unlikely Latin

Be careful – some species don't seem to have proper Latin names at all, or are saddled with rather unfortunate ones:

Maidenhair Tree (*Ginkgo biloba*)
Mistle Thrush (*Turdus viscivorus*)

Trinomial names

Sub-species are accorded a third name to distinguish them from other sub-species or from the species of which they are a sub-species. Here are a couple that manage a doubling up, so at least you have to recall only two of the three names, and a triple-barrelled (or, more properly, *trinomial*) name sounds very impressive when tripped off to an expectant audience.

Red Grouse (*Lagopus lagopus scoticus*) – a sub-species of the Willow Grouse

Common Wolf (*Canis lupus lupus*) – a sub-species of the Grey Wolf

EASY NATURE

Just remember this:

If you dedicate yourself to memorising only one Latin name, the Black Rat is probably the easiest of the lot, for it is *Rattus rattus*.

- In 1933, German entomologist Oscar Scheibel discovered a blind cave beetle that preys on cave-dwellers smaller than itself. He named it *Anophthalmus hitleri*, in honour of the then German Chancellor (there is some debate today as to whether this was a backhanded insult or not). The beetle is in such demand from current-day Nazi sympathisers that it has almost been collected to extinction, and is now found in only a handful of caves in Slovenia.

- Two American entomologists, Dr Kelly B. Miller and Dr Quentin D. Wheeler, have added *Agathidium bushi*, *Agathidium cheneyi* and *Agathidium rumsfeldi* to the canon of binomial names – an act they claim to be a genuine homage to the three American politicians, despite the fact that the trio of species in question are slime mould beetles.

- Latin was chosen for naming living things because the language was the lingua franca of Europe in the 18th century, much like English is today.

- An *x* in the middle of a binomial name signifies that the species is a *hybrid* form. Thus the Weeping Willow – a cross between the White Willow and Peking Willow – is rendered *Salix x chrysocoma*.

What you should say:

'Strictly speaking, old chap, it was the Visigoths rather than Latin that killed off the Romans, you know.'

The language of flowers

Y ou may have always thought that a gift of flowers has no greater significance beyond 'I love you', 'Happy Mother's Day', or 'I'm sorry I sat on your hamster'. Not so. Flowers have been imbued with meanings far beyond this limited range for thousands of years. For instance, the ancient Greeks attached a story to practically any flower they came across: Anemones were drops of blood that had dripped from the body of the dying Adonis; the Rhododendron was a nymph whose kiss could kill a man; and the Narcissus was the metamorphosis of the youth who had rejected Echo's love and had thus been punished by being made to fall in love with his own reflection. Although today we rarely make such connections, the word 'narcissistic' is still going strong, and a gift of Narcissi to someone who tends to self-obsession might well connote something more than the customary expressions of love or sympathy, or an appeal for forgiveness.

British flower language

The early decades of the 20th century were the golden years of British flower language. Mimicking the Greeks, the British gave each bloom a specific meaning, most of which were based on some whim or fancy, although a few did attempt a logical association of ideas (for example, a gift of Nettles meant 'You are spiteful') or borrowed from earlier times (an Olive branch in a bouquet meant 'Peace'). A tiny portfolio called simply *The Language of Flowers* was produced by the venerable publishers Frederick Warne & Co. in an attempt to catalogue the 700 or so flowers and other plants that had been accorded a distinct meaning by that time. There follows a selection to get you started.

Your first 30 flower words

Basil	*Hatred*
Birdsfoot Trefoil	*Revenge*
Bluebell	*Constancy or Sorrowful regret*
Camellia Japonica (white)	*Perfected loveliness*
Carnation (deep red)	*Alas! for my poor heart*
Carnation (pink)	*Woman's love*
Carnation (yellow)	*Disdain*

Crocus	*Abuse not*
Deadly Nightshade	*Falsehood*
Hawthorn	*Hope*
Horseshoe-leaf Geranium	*Stupidity*
Jasmine	*Amiability*
Larkspur	*Levity*

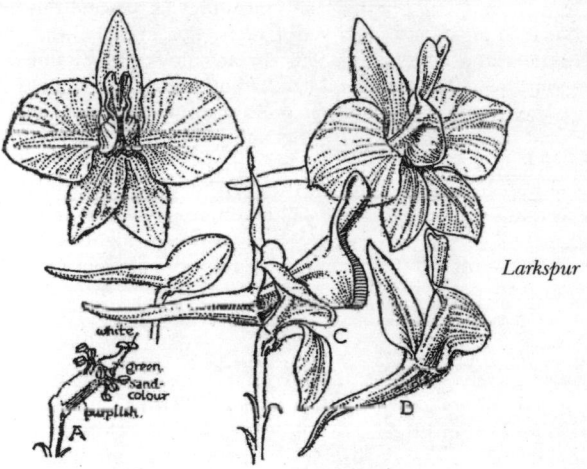

Larkspur

Lavender	*Distrust*
Lettuce	*Cold-heartedness*
Lichen	*Dejection or Solitude*
Lily of the Valley	*Return of happiness*
Marigold	*Grief*
Marigold (French)	*Jealousy*
Moss	*Maternal love*
Peach blossom	*I am your captive*
Rose	*Love*
Sorrel	*Wit ill-timed*
Thistle	*Austerity*
Thrift	*Sympathy*
Traveller's Joy	*Safety*
Tulip (red)	*Declaration of love*
Violet (blue)	*Faithfulness*
Woodbine	*Fraternal love*
Zinnia	*Thoughts of absent friends*

The language of flowers *cont.*

Woodbine

Some curiosities

Chilean Bellflower	*There is no unalloyed good*
Clarkia	*The variety of your conversation delights me*
Currant	*Thy frown will kill me*
Japanese Rose	*Beauty is your only attraction*
Locust Tree (green)	*Affection from beyond the grave*
Persimmon	*Bury me amid Nature's beauties*
Tansy	*I declare war against you*

Putting together whole sentences

By carefully assembling a bouquet of mixed flowers, the sender is able to express quite complex ideas. Thus, **London Pride** (Frivolity), **Lobelia** (Malevolence) and **Laburnum** (Forsaken) sent together would apparently convey the message: 'Your frivolity and malevolence will cause you to be forsaken by all.'

Playing around with the concepts

According to *The Language of Flowers*, 'Place a marigold on its head, and it signifies "Mental anguish."' Think back to your state of mind the last time you put a **Marigold** on its head and you will find the book is quite right. Bend a flower to the right when giving it and it means *I*, bend to the left for *you*. If you wish to add an *I am*, twist a **Laurel** leaf around the bouquet. Add a folded **Ivy** leaf for *I have*; or a **Virginia Creeper** leaf for *I offer you*. The receiver should kiss the flowers to say *Yes*, or throw away a petal for *No*.

EASY NATURE

Just remember this:

Having a bouquet of **Gum Rockroses** (*Cistus ladanifer*) delivered to a loved one sends the message 'I shall die tomorrow', which may be thought melodramatic if it turns out that you make it through the following 24 hours. You may get a better reaction by sending chocolates.

• The memorable Interflora advertising campaign which called upon the public to 'Say it with flowers' led to the equally famous graffito: 'Say it with flowers ... send her a triffid.'

What you should say:

'Unfortunately, the shop was all out of Clarkia so can I just say that the variety of your conversation delights me?'

How to predict the weather

Anyone who has lived in Britain for more than 24 hours cannot fail to be aware that the weather is distinctly changeable. The Meteorological Office does its best but they're on a hiding to nothing really, since anyone who predicts what the weather will do in more than a few hours' time is likely to be undone by the caprices of the winds and the weather systems that glide about the globe. Being able to do a little forecasting yourself when out and about is therefore not just a party trick but actually a very useful skill, and perhaps even a life-saving one. There thus follows a variety of means by which you may be able to anticipate what the skies have in store over the following few hours. Of course, if you can consult several at the same time, and they all agree, there is an even greater chance that they are right.

Indicators of rain

Insect-eating birds

Flying insects tend to fly lower when rain is due. Although they themselves may be too small to see, you can tell where they are by the behaviour of insect-eating birds such as Swallows (p. 148). If the birds are flying low (in search of insects) there is a good chance that rain is imminent.

The wind

A change in the weather is also indicated by the wind picking up on an otherwise fine day.

Cows

It doesn't always work, but when cows are seen to sit down en masse, it is often a sign that rain is on the way.

Bonfires

Smoke from a bonfire that swirls or appears to get knocked down after rising a little above the fire is a sign that rain, and possibly a storm, are coming.

Vegetation

Pine cones open and close depending on the levels of humidity. An open cone indicates dry weather, while rain or fog is forecast by a closed cone. The Carline Thistle (*Carlina vulgaris*) has flowers that act in much the same way. The flowers of the Scarlet Pimpernel (p. 93) close when the weather is about to take a turn for the worse. Vegetation also smells more just before rainfall.

Sound

Sound carries further before it starts to rain.

Dry weather ahead

Seaweed

Hang a piece of Bootlace Weed (*Chorda filum*) – otherwise known as Mermaid's Tresses – in a sheltered spot. When the humidity is low, the seaweed becomes dry and brittle, meaning it is likely that the next day will be a dry one.

Reading the clouds

- Low, dark clouds with an anvil-shaped top (Cumulonimbus) are the precursor to a storm, strong winds and possibly hail.

- Fluffy white clouds (Cumulus) presage rain only when numerous and close together.

- High, rippled clouds (Cirrocumulus) will soon disperse, leaving a clear sky.

- Many people claim that they feel arthritic or rheumatic twinges, or pain in the corns on their feet, before a cold snap or wet weather. While it is true that arthritis and rheumatism are exacerbated by a drop in temperature, there is no scientific proof that such aches and pains can *foretell* a cold or wet spell.

EASY NATURE

Just remember this:

Red sky at night – shepherds' delight.
Red sky in morning – shepherds' warning.[1]

What you should say:

'If you can see Manchester from half a mile away, it's going to rain; if you can't, it *is* raining.'

---

[1] Red sunsets come about only when there is not much moisture in the air, making it unlikely that it will rain the next day; whereas a red sunrise often heralds a storm.

A Select Bibliography and Webography

Books

Birds of Britain and Europe, Jim Flegg; New Holland, 1992

Birdwatching, Rob Hume; HarperCollins 2005

Butterflies and Moths, Paul Sterry and Andrew MacKay; Dorling Kindersley, 2004

Britain's Wildlife, Plants and Flowers, ed. Michael Wright; Reader's Digest, 1987

Complete British Animals, Paul Sterry; Collins, 2005

Complete British Wildlife, Paul Sterry; Collins, 1997

Encyclopaedia of Insects and Invertebrates, Maurice Burton and Robert Burton; Little, Brown, 2002

Field Guide to the Trees of Britain, Europe and North America, Andrew Cleave; The Crowood Press, 1994

Food for Free, Richard Mabey; HarperCollins, 2004

Food from the Wild, Ian Burrows; New Holland, 2005

Guide to Freshwater Fish of Britain and Europe, Peter S. Maitland and Keith Linsell; Philip's, 2006

How to See Nature, Frances Pitt; B.T. Batsford Ltd, 1940

How to Watch Wildlife, Bill Oddie; Collins, 2005

Insects, Spiders and Other Terrestrial Arthropods, George C. McGavin; Dorling Kindersley, 2000

Mushrooms, Thomas Læssøe; Dorling Kindersley, 1998

RSPB Birds of Britain and Europe, Rob Hume; Dorling Kindersley, 2002

SAS Survival Guide, John Wiseman; Collins, 2004

Shells, S. Peter Dance; Dorling Kindersley, 1992

The Trees that Made Britain, Archie Miles; BBC Books, 2006

The Language of Flowers, Kate Greenaway; Frederick Warne & Co., no date

Trees, Allen Coombes; Dorling Kindersley, 2004

Trees, Alastair Fitter; HarperCollins, 2002

Wild Animals, Chris Gibson; Dorling Kindersley, 2005

Websites

Badger Pages by Steve Jackson:
www.badgers.org.uk/badgerpages/index.html

British Arachnological Society (for all things spidery):
www.britishspiders.org.uk

British Butterflies by Steven Cheshire (one of the most
alluring sites on the internet):
www.britishbutterflies.co.uk

British Dragonfly Society:
www.dragonflysoc.org.uk

British Wild Boar by Dr Martin Goulding:
www.britishwildboar.org.uk

Conchological Society of Great Britain and Ireland:
www.conchsoc.org

EDGE List:
www.edgeofexistence.org

IUCN Red List of Threatened Species:
www.iucnredlist.org

Royal Society for the Protection of Birds:
www.rspb.org

ACKNOWLEDGEMENTS

The author would like to express his appreciation to the following people for their kind help with the research for this book:

Caroline Delves, Pablo Stockley, Caroline McCormick, Kim Peat, Anna and Caith Kushner, Lizzie's mum, Flt. Lt. (ret.) Christopher 'Bimbo' Hanson, Priscilla and Martin Euden, Gail Dinner, Hazel and Geoff Wills, Katy 'cemeteries-a-go-go' Nicholson, Claire Ellis, Miriam Hargreaves, Sarah Pistol, Carey Bowtell, Cathy McCann, George Mahoney, Martin X, Andy Jones, Clive 'through the chicane' Wills, and Elisabeth 'Rhinos R Me' Whitebread.

Dulce et decorum est pro tuo scriptore indigena mori.[1]

---

[1] It is a sweet and noble thing to die for your local author.

GLOSSARY

Naturalists tend to use terminology that is not the stuff of everyday conversation among the public at large. To get you onto an even footing, here are a few words to learn for the next time a naturalist bandies them about in your direction.

(NB. All words in the following definitions that are also included in this glossary in their own right are given in *italics*.)

Abdomen – the section of a *vertebrate* creature that contains the stomach and other organs.

Ament – another term for a *catkin*.

Anther – the top bit of the *stamen*.

Barbel – a whiskery feeler projecting from the lips or jaws of a fish.

Binomial – the scientific name of a living thing (*bi-* = two, *-nomial* = name), always given in Latin, with just the first name capitalised (e.g. the binomial name for humans is *Homo sapiens*).

Bio-diversity – the range of organisms that can be found in any given ecological community.

Biomass – the total quantity or weight of living organisms in a given area.

Bivalve – a class of *molluscs* with shells formed of two pieces.

Bract – a small modified leaf (often a scale-like structure) underneath a flower.

Brush – a Fox's tail.

Byssus – a tuft of silky threads produced by some *molluscs*.

Calyx – a ring of (often green) *sepals* that protects the flower bud.

Carapace – the hard upper shell of a *crustacean*.

Catkin – a furry cluster (usually drooping) of minute leaves and petal-less flowers produced by some trees.

Cetaceans – an order of *mammals* that includes whales, dolphins and porpoises (but *not* sharks, which are fish).

Conifer – a tree that produces cones (such as Pines, Firs, Larches, Yews etc).

Coppicing – a method of managing woodland in which trees are cut down to their stumps in order to encourage thick growths of thin poles.

Corolla – the collective name for the petals of a flower that form a ring (and are protected by a ring of *sepals*).

Crustacean – a member of the large Crustacea group that includes crabs, lobsters, woodlice and many others.

Deciduous – a way of describing any woody plant that loses its leaves in winter.

Diaphoretic – herbs (or other substances) that can be used to induce sweating.

Entomologist – someone who studies the forms and behaviour of insects.

Evergreen – a plant that retains its leaves the whole year.

Fairy ring – a circle of fungi.

Felid – any animal belonging to the cat family.

Feral – any animal that has returned to the wild (or whose ancestors have returned to the wild) after a period of domestication.

Filament – the stalk that supports the *anther*.

Floret – a flowerhead containing many separate flowers.

Form – a shallow pit used by Hares.

Gastropod – (lit. 'stomach-footed') a class of *molluscs*, each of which have a head that includes eyes and tentacles, a foot (just one) and a shell consisting of one piece (or occasionally no shell at all).

Genus – a class of related *species* (plural form: genera).

Hybrid – the offspring of two different parent species.

Invertebrate – any animal with no backbone (see also *vertebrate*).

Larva – the soft, worm-like immature form of certain insects.

Lobe – a rounded segment of a leaf.

Mammal – a class of *vertebrate* animals in which the female suckles offspring with milk secreted from her body.

Mollusc – an *invertebrate* creature with a soft body and no legs, which usually forms a shell.

Mossery – a place to keep a collection of moss.

Mustelid – any member of the weasel family (such as Weasels, Badgers, Otters, Stoats etc).

Mycology – the study of fungi.

Nestling – a young bird that has not yet left the nest.

Noseleaf – a flat section over a bat's nasal area that is used for broadcasting and receiving ultrasonic signals.

Ovary – in plants, the lower section of the *pistil* and the part that ripens into a fruit.

Pistil – a flower's female reproductive parts, including the *ovary*, *style* and *stigma*.

Pneumostome – the pore on the right-hand side of certain slugs through which they are able to breathe.

Pollen – the powdery substance produced by *anthers* that contains the male reproductive cells.

Pupa – an insect between the larval and adult stages of its life (also called the chrysalis).

Rhizoid – a thin root-hair produced by mosses, liverworts and ferns that takes in nourishment.

Sepal – a modified leaf, a ring of which form the *calyx.*

Species – animals or plants that resemble each other and can produce offspring.

Spore – a minute (usually single-celled) reproductive body produced by seedless plants (such as fungi); it is dispersed and grows into a new organism.

Spur – a lateral shoot from a plant's branch or stem.

Stamen – a flower's male reproductive organ (usually including a *filament* and an *anther*).

Stigma – the upper part of a flower's *pistil*, designed to receive *pollen.*

Style – an extension of the *ovary*, it is the part of a flower's female reproductive structure (*pistil*) that supports the *stigma.*

Taxon – any of the groups such as species, genus, family, class, order, etc. by which living things are classified.

Thorax – the middle section of the body of an insect, arachnid or *crustacean.*

Umbel – an umbrella-like flowerhead.

Ungulate – any animal that has hoofs.

Vertebrate – any animal with a backbone.

Vespid – any member of the Vespidae family (including wasps and hornets)

Wattle – a loose fold of skin hanging from some part of the head of certain lizards or birds (typically from the throat, but the Red Grouse has a wattle above its eye).

Wildfowl – a bird hunted by humans for food or sport.

Withers – the ridge between the shoulder blades of a horse, marking the highest point of its back.

INDEX

Page numbers in bold indicate the main entry for each subject